Architecting Growth in the Digital Era

Stefan Henningsson • Gustav Normark Toppenberg

Architecting Growth in the Digital Era

How to Exploit Enterprise Architecture
to Enable Corporate Acquisitions

 Springer

Stefan Henningsson
Department of Digitalization
Copenhagen Business School
Frederiksberg, Denmark

Gustav Normark Toppenberg
Janus Insights, LLC
Chicago, IL, USA

ISBN 978-3-030-39481-3   ISBN 978-3-030-39482-0   (eBook)
https://doi.org/10.1007/978-3-030-39482-0

This Springer imprint is published by the registered company Springer Nature Switzerland AG.
The registered company address is: Gewerbestrasse 11, 6330 Cham, Switzerland

From Stefan: To Nina

*From Gustav: To my wife Johanna,
my daughters Camilla and Vivienne and
my parents*

Preface

This book is the result of an ongoing journey. A journey that we began some 15 years ago and still continue into today. This journey has taken us to places we did not know existed and given us insights we had no idea that we needed when we started. We have met with industrious and clever people that have enlightened our perceptions. We have heard about challenges and solutions. We have witnessed success and failure. We have met with engaged managers that have been willing to listen to our ideas, and we have had the opportunity to put our thoughts into practice to learn what problems they solve—and which they do not solve.

For Stefan, the journey started back in 2004 when he got the opportunity to do a PhD at Lund University, Sweden. The PhD project was a collaboration with the university and a large industrial company that was seeking to transform itself through an extensive acquisition program. For 4 years, Stefan studied the IT challenges of acquisition integration and wrote his PhD thesis titled "Managing Information Systems Integration in Corporate Acquisitions." The thesis was essentially a 400-page documentation of all things that can go wrong in the IT integration of two companies. When he graduated, Stefan thought he had pretty much figured out what was going on. It turned out that he had much more to learn.

Stefan continued his research on the topic at Copenhagen Business School, Denmark. First as a postdoc, then as an assistant professor, associate professor, and eventually as a professor in the Department of Digitalization. A PhD became a career.

Copenhagen in Denmark is probably the best place in the world for this kind of research. Denmark is among the more digitized countries in the world and Danish companies are very progressive when it comes to leveraging all sorts of digital technologies to compete internationally. Denmark is also a very small country with a great degree of communal responsibility for education and research. In Copenhagen, a meeting with a C-suite executive to discuss acquisition aspirations and challenges is typically only a short bike ride away.

The work at Copenhagen Business School took Stefan inside well-renowned Danish companies such as Maersk, Danske Bank, Carlsberg, and Danisco and extended to international collaborations with companies such as SAP and Siemens.

This work led to further insights on what some of these companies managed to accomplish in the IT integration that most of their peers did not. The work also put light on the fact that for most of the companies acquisition was just one of many types of ongoing organizational transformation activities taking place in parallel work streams. While important in themselves, acquisitions were still only one aspect of an ongoing organizational transformation.

Gustav started his journey towards this book following his family to Minneapolis, MN, in the USA as his father managed the integration of the acquisition of Advance Machine Company by Nilfisk, an international supplier of cleaning equipment headquartered in Denmark. Following in the traces of Nilfisk's expansion in the US market, Gustav made the USA his new home as a student at the Metropolitan State University in Saint Paul, Minnesota. He then continued to do an MBA in Global Management at the Thunderbird School of Global Management, while at the same time kicking off his professional career at Hilti, a Liechtenstein-based multinational company that produces machinery for the construction industry.

After finishing his MBA, Gustav relocated to the bay area and continued his career at Cisco. At Cisco, Gustav got introduced to the discipline of Enterprise Architecture (EA) and got to head a group on EA operations and governance.

Then, our roads crossed as Gustav made the decision to pursue a PhD. While comfortable executing EA frameworks in practice, he aspired to earn a greater understanding of how these practices practically contributed to the strategic development of a company. Acting on this need, he started a conversation with Copenhagen Business School about the possibility to deepen the understanding of EA and why it had becomes such an important practice in contemporary business. This put Gustav in contact with Stefan and after a series of conversations, we both agreed that there ought to be some interesting connection between EA and acquisitions. At this point we were driven more by intuition than real-world evidence. The two concepts seemed to fit somehow because they were both about change processes that involved both business strategy and technological enablement, but we were unsure about how the connection would materialize.

With Stefan as part of the supervising team, Gustav spent three years exploring the connection. Synthesizing input from a number of companies in the USA and in Europe, Gustav conceptually addressed the technology-related challenges of this form of growth and detailed EA's role in enabling this practice. After three years, Gustav successfully defended his PhD titled "Innovation-based Mergers and Acquisitions," in which EA was positioned as a key enabler to address the specific challenges of complementing internal innovation with the acquisitions of innovative start-ups.

In subsequent work, we have enriched our understanding of the intersection of acquisitions and EA by looking also at more traditional acquisitions, driven by business opportunities such as scale and scope. We have looked across industries and geographies. We have contrasted and compared the use of EA practices in nascent stages with their more elaborated peers. And we have moved from the deep explanatory focus of PhD students on why things happen to the managerial practices of making things happen. In his roles of heading EA for several large, international businesses, Gustav has been part of putting the ideas into practice, learning about the obstacles on his way, but also witnessed the value brought.

At first glance, the two concepts of acquisition and EA appear paradoxical to their nature. Acquisitions are all about dynamic change and speed. EA's goal is that every element of a company, being business- or technology-related, fit together into a coherent whole. Stability makes the life on an architect simple. Acquisitions are typically driven by a short-sighted focus with immediate payoff, particularly in those that aim at speeding up innovation to catch up on or move ahead of competition. A key contribution of EA is the long-term consistency of the technological landscape. So, at first look, acquisitions and EA seem like an odd match. But, it is of course the very distinct natures that make the concepts essential to combine. Combining them gives an opportunity to balance a business that excels today, without compromising tomorrow!

In a bigger picture, learning how to run today's business without compromising the business of tomorrow is a key challenge that companies need to master as part of transforming to the new digital era of business. Because, digital transformation is not about transforming a company from one stable state to another. At its heart, digital transformation is about reinventing the company to be able to cope with continuous change, without compromising momentary excellence. Digital technologies enable changes in customer interaction and production processes, in supplier relations and partner collaborations, in business models and in the complete configuration of value-creating logics and stakeholder roles in the market. Because of digital technologies, old industries are being disrupted or are converging with other industries. New industries emerge, where, at least initially, it is very unclear what the dominant value propositions will be and which actors are going to dominate in the end. So, companies need to be geared towards constant change in the digital era.

But, constant change brings little value if it cannot be combined with momentary excellence. What good does it do to be the first into a new, emerging market unless you can also set up an efficient business in the new market? It is not that the old ideas on operational efficiency are not valid anymore. Efficiency is still good, but it is not everything. Being entrenched in a highly efficient state will not do the job, when the rules of the game are changing. So, if you want, you can read the book as one example of what it takes to balance the need for ongoing transformation with a business practice that in every moment also delivers operational excellence.

What we have tried to accomplish with this book is to express our current thoughts about why acquisitions and EA need to be combined and how to do it. Thoughts that have been inspired by numerous empirical studies and trialed in practice.

The target audience for this book is threefold:

- EA managers that are looking to broaden the use of EA in their organizations, or to create the rationale for further developments in the EA capability.

- Acquisition and other transformation managers that face the increasing complexity of acquiring and integrating new businesses in the continuously more digitized world.
- Students, both at master's and executive level, that are interested in a real-world application of EA that matters to companies or more broadly want to understand what it takes to reinvent a company for competition in the digital age.

In practical terms, we present the content of the book as follows. First, to set the scene, the introduction in Chap. 1 explains how digitalization is the root cause of paradoxical development where the need for acquisition-based growth is increasing, at the same time as realizing the value from acquisitions is more difficult than ever. Exploiting EA for this purpose is a key enabler of acquisitive growth in the digital era.

The rest of the book is then divided into three parts. Part I develops the fundament for the book by decomposing the problem of acquisitive growth and explaining how advancements in EA practices have created the potential for mitigating the challenges. Chapter 2 introduces the reader to the acquisition challenge, specifically the rationales, outcomes, and process steps of corporate acquisitions. Chapter 3 describes the features of an advanced EA capability, including the enablers of the holistic and engaged qualities.

In Part II, the following four chapters detail how an advanced EA capability can be engaged in and contribute to the different phases of an acquisition process. Chapter 4 addresses how EA can contribute to the preparation for acquisition by *positioning* an organization to be ready to be an acquirer. Chapter 5 explains how the engagement of EA in the selection of acquisition targets can support the acquirer to accurately *identify* the business value of the acquisition. Chapter 6 defines the capacity of EA to *direct* work in the integration phase to increase integration efficiency, avoiding the incremental accumulation of inefficiencies hampering future growth. Chapter 7 portrays the potential of using EA in the post-integration business continuation phase by *monitoring* progress and the corrections of "organizational debt" taken to effectuate short-term acquisition benefits.

At last, in Part III, three chapters provide hands-on guidance for how to start engaging EA in the acquisition process. Chapter 8 discusses how to activate EA in the acquisition process given a specific *capacity to perform*. Chapter 9 addresses how you *get your foot in the door and beyond*. This chapter presents where to start the journey and how to move onwards to unlock the full capacity of EA. Finally, Chap. 10 provides some concluding words and personal advice from the authors as *notes for the journey* ahead.

Taken together, these ten chapters are aimed to equip you as a reader with cognitive keys and practical guidelines to manage acquisitive growth in the digital era. Then, your job is to adapt them to your context. We do not claim to serve you a recipe for universal success. For that, acquisitions are way too multifaceted and EA practices too complex.

What we write should be interpreted in an actual context, in light of what it takes to run a successful business of your kind and with the premises for EA in your organization. Fifteen years of studies on this topic has taught us that no two situations are exactly the same. What it takes to create success in one situation is never exactly the same as in the next. But our experience has taught us that pure luck has surprisingly little to do with success. Instead, what creates success are clever and hard-working individuals that act through effective tools, based on a solid understanding of the problem at hand.

While we cannot make you clever or hard-working, we can contribute to that you get the cognitive keys to understand and the practical tools to enact EA in the context of corporate acquisitions. This is why we have written this book. We hope that you will enjoy reading it and put it to practice in your organization. And when you do, let us know, because our journey has been going on for 15 years and still counting!

Copenhagen, Denmark   Stefan Henningsson
Chicago, IL, USA   Gustav Normark Toppenberg
November, 2019

Acknowledgments

Many organizations and individuals have contributed generously with their time and resources to the work underpinning this book. We are particularly grateful to the companies and the managers that have allowed us to study their practices and to test our ideas. We are also appreciative of our colleagues that in formal or informal roles have reviewed our work and provided constructive feedback on how to express our ideas. Furthermore, we would like to extend our appreciation to our current and past employers that have supported our work on this topic. Finally, a very special thank-you goes to our families that have enabled us to venture on this project. Without the contribution from any of you, this book would not have existed. We are immensely grateful for your support.

Contents

1   Acquisitions: The New Game for Enterprise Architecture   1
      References   6

Part I   Framing the Issue

2   The Acquisition Challenge   9
      Acquisition Types   10
      Acquisition Outcomes   15
      The Acquisition Process   17
      Chapter Key Points   19
      References   20

3   The Advanced Enterprise Architecture Capability   21
      Purposes   24
      Qualities   25
      The Holistic Quality   25
         The Engaged Quality   26
      Capacities   27
         People   28
         Processes   28
         Technology   29
      Artifacts   31
         Transformation Models   31
         Solution Models   35
      Chapter Key Points   38
      References   38

Part II   Enterprise Architecture in the Acquisition Process

4   Preparation: *Positioning* the Organization   41
      Infrastructure Preparation   45

Documentation   48
Knowledge Integration   49
Gap Exposure   50
Platformization   50
Chapter Key Points   51
References   52

5   **Target Selection:** *Identifying* **Value**   53
Business Case Estimation   54
Transformation Needs Assessment   58
Identification of Roadblocks   59
Reverse Integration Potential   60
Suite Analysis   62
Platform Consistency Modelling   63
Identification of Nontransferable Enablers   64
Chapter Key Points   64
References   65

6   **Integration:** *Direct* **Work Streams**   67
Refined To-Be State Definition   69
Organizational Design   70
IT Enablement   71
Roadmap Development   73
Carve-Out Bridging   74
Chapter Key Points   75
References   76

7   **Continuation:** *Monitoring* **Progression**   77
Integration Evaluation   78
Elimination of Integration Debt   81
Chapter Key Points   83
References   84

Part III   Back at the Office

8   **Your Capacity to Perform**   87
Understanding Your EA Maturity   87
Traditional EA: Documenting the Technical Transformation   90
Active EA: Defining the Technical Transformation   91
Aspirational EA: Informing the Organizational Transformation   93
Advanced EA: Orchestrating the Organizational Transformation   94
Chapter Key Points   96
Reference   96

9   **Getting Your Foot in the Door and Beyond**   97
Entry: Get Started   97
Increasing Engagement: Capacity and Mandate   100
Chapter Key Points   102

10   A Note for the Journey   105
       Acquisitions Can Mean a Breakthrough for Enterprise Architecture . . .   105
       EA Is About Having Fewer Problems and Better Solutions   107
       Principles for Introducing EA in Acquisitions   107
       Grow with the Digital Challenge   109
       We've Seen Nothing Yet   110

About the Authors

Stefan Henningsson is Professor at Copenhagen Business School, Denmark, where he researches strategic management of IT resources. Dr. Henningsson completed his PhD at the School of Economics and Management at Lund University, Sweden, with a thesis on the management of IT integration in corporate mergers and acquisitions. He has researched how companies such as Cisco Systems, SAP, AON, Danske Bank, Lego, Maersk Line, and many others manage their growth strategies in the digital era. Dr. Henningsson has published more than 100 peer-refereed academic papers in leading academic journals as well as more practitioner-oriented journals. He teaches subjects that include digital transformation and digital platform strategies to executive learners, and IT strategy to master-level students. Dr. Henningsson is also the coordinator of the IT management master-level education and Digitalization concentration manager in the Executive MBA program at Copenhagen Business School, as well as a member of the Danish IT Association's Council for IT Strategy.

Gustav Normark Toppenberg is an Enterprise Transformation Executive with 20+ years of experience. His background includes building and leading transformational efforts for both small and global companies with a focus on business, data, and digital domains. His professional experience includes executive roles in Enterprise Architecture, Lean Agile Product Delivery, Advanced Data & Analytics and M&A at Boston Consulting Group (BCG), Catalina Marketing, Aon Plc, and Cisco Systems. His academic experience teaching and publishing practitioner includes roles as an Adjunct Professor at Loyola University Chicago—Quinlan School of Business and as an Adjunct Professor at UC Berkeley in the areas of Advanced Analytics/AI, Emerging Technology, Design Thinking, and Lean Agile.

Chapter 1
Acquisitions: The New Game for Enterprise Architecture

To unlock the full potential of Enterprise Architecture (EA), it needs a context that is of relevance to the firm. EA as a practice has been around for some time now. From the early attempts in the 1980s when EA attracted the interest of pioneers searching to form a holistic grip on firms' growing the technological landscape, EA has become a well-established practice in the business community. Global and local EA conferences attract thousands of practitioners, and the best universities and business schools have incorporated EA into their curriculum. EA has matured into a fully developed discipline, with a set of mental models and practical tools that together form a sophisticated framework for orchestrating organizational transformation. The fact that almost all large companies have embraced some sort of EA function reflects the need of the digital age to think holistically about change across the different layers of an organization in business.

Yet, despite the growing and prospering EA community, many EA leaders struggle with getting recognition of the value that EA brings to the organization. One key reason for this is that EA is essential for the long-term health of a company, but rarely links directly to organizational performance indicators that are measured on a quarterly basis. EA typically paves the way for rapid product development, new market entry, or process innovation, but the impact of EA on measured outcomes is indirect, through complex nests of the activities that EA supports. EA rarely gets to claim its victory. As a consequence, EA struggles to get recognition of its contributions, to attract resources to develop its full potential, and to earn the mandate to drive organizational transformations.

The challenge to establish the value of the EA function and to grow its potential can be addressed by putting EA in a context that is relevant to the firm. Corporate acquisition is such a context. In fact, an acquisition is one of the rare situations where the *full* capacity of EA as a transformative tool comes into play and stands out as a key enabler of strategic aspirations. The challenge of acquiring companies plays directly into the strength of EA and the ability of a skilled EA function to orchestrate a complex organizational transformation that cuts across business and technology

© Springer Nature Switzerland AG 2020
S. Henningsson, G. N. Toppenberg, *Architecting Growth in the Digital Era*,
https://doi.org/10.1007/978-3-030-39482-0_1

layers. Through EA, acquiring companies can become both more effective in dealing with the problems and also ensure that they have fewer problems in the first place.

For more than a century, mergers and acquisitions have been popular means for executing corporate strategy. This is true today more than ever. Since 2000, almost 800,000 deals have been reported worldwide (IMAA 2019). In 2018 alone, more than 52,000 deals were reported, corresponding to a total deal value of more than US \$4 trillion (IMAA 2019). Appropriately executed, acquisitions enable business benefits of scale and scope, give access to unique resources and support strategic renewal. In practice, however, acquisition benefits are illusive and difficult to materialize. Reports in the trade press, data from consultancy firms, and investigations by researchers indicate that 60–80% of acquisitions in the private sector destroy rather than create financial value as measured by short-term performance, long-term performance, and firm value. In some cases, corporate acquisitions have been devastating for both firms (King et al. 2004, 2017).

Because of the extreme variations in performance, acquisitions are where careers are made—or broken. When Maersk Lines, the world's largest container shipping company, acquired its competitor P&O Nedlloyd, "botched IT integration" led to that the company losing its tracks of containers and could not invoice customers for several months (Financial Times 2007). In 18 months, the combined global market share fell from 18% to 14%, and the merged organization lost 25% of its customers. No executive survives such destruction of shareholder value, and individuals that are associated with the failure are likely to be dragged along in the process. In fact, more than 47% of all CEOs are replaced within five years after an acquisition (Lehn and Zhao 2006).

The high values at stake in acquisitions have made the support of acquisitive growth a billion-dollar industry. Financial advisors to guide companies in their decision-making, legal bureaus to investigate regulative ramifications and help respond to concerns of competition authorities, specialized firm brokers to connect divestures and start-ups with prospective acquirers, and management consultancies to help direct and provide the manpower for acquirers see through the enactment of deals. Through these firms, decades of experiences have been formalized into invaluable resources such as playbooks, structured methodologies, and actionable guidelines that represent the very best practices of the past.

However, it is important to stress that these are the best practices of the *past*—not the best practice for how to deal with *future* acquisitions. As business practices and global conditions for business evolve, so do the challenges to and solutions for value creating acquisitions. One particularly critical aspect of the evolving conditions for business is that companies have become deeply dependent on their enabling digital technologies. The tech-wave has been going on for a while now. The term Web 2.0 gained popularity in 2004 to represent an increasing democratization of the internet, with the emergence of Wikipedia, Facebook, Twitter, and other platforms for distributed content creation. Innovations in mobile technologies, such as the smartphone, fundamentally altered our communication patterns. Already several decades ago digital technologies became indispensable enablers for companies to do business. In the last decade, this wave of digitization picked up its pace.

Today, however, the technology wave has not only continued to accelerate, but has also changed in its very nature. Technology trends such as robotic process automation (RPA), Internet of Things (IoT), edge computing, cloud/virtualization, blockchain, big data and data analytics, artificial intelligence (AI) and advanced machine learning, 3D printing, and ambient technological networks are radically transforming almost every industry. This transformation is evidenced by the fact that digital technologies are no longer just supporting how companies do business— *digital is becoming the way to do business.*

For acquisitions, the ongoing digital transformation has two implications. One is that acquisitions are becoming an increasingly important means for corporate strategy. Research shows that the speed of change in an industry is directly correlated to the degree of digitization. Digitalization means that firms can push out product and process innovation faster, reap economies of scale from critical enabling infrastructures, and orchestrate complex product scopes into complete solutions (Brynjolfsson and McAfee 2014). This diminishes the importance of the notion of sustained competitive advantage, if not rendering it completely obsolete. Instead, strategists talk about "dog eat dog" markets, where firms that leverage innovations can quickly dominate the market, and just as easily be dethroned by a rival with a new approach. To keep up with the speed of change, corporate acquisitions are indispensable as they can rapidly fuel the relentless transformation.

Paradoxically, the other implication of digitization is that realizing the value from acquisitions is more difficult than ever (Fig. 1.1). McKinsey estimates that 45–60% of the expected business benefits from acquisitions are directly dependent on the integration of enabling technologies (Sarrazin and West 2011). Because of the increasing fusion between business and technology strategies, to substantiate acquisition benefits, acquiring firms need to manage organizational change across the different business and technological layers of the organization in a synchronous way. A Gartner study found that technological integration typically accounted for about 25% of the total integration costs in acquisitions (Gartner 2016). This is, however, of minor importance compared to the enabling or disruptive effect the technological integration can have on the combined business organization.

According to a survey by Accenture, technological integration is the second most important reason for acquisition failures (Accenture 2006). Technology integration

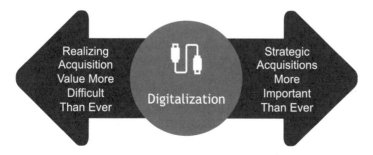

Fig. 1.1 The paradoxical effect of digitalization on corporate acquisitions

does not cause failures because the cost of integration dwarfs the business benefits, but because the way technology is integrated does not enable the realization of merger benefits or because short-term solutions induce misalignment between the business and technology layers. Over time, these misalignments cumulatively add to organizational complexities, and as a result it becomes cumbersome, or even impossible, to exploit digital opportunities. Therefore, today, any prospective acquirer needs to direct their attention to the challenge of how to orchestrate the change that acquisition brings about across the business and technology layers.

We believe that at the heart of the ability to manage an ongoing and multilayered organizational transformation rests an advanced EA capability with a specific charter to act as a transformation engine connecting strategic intent and execution excellence. Our take on EA, based on research and first-hand experiences of acquisition-based growth, have taught us that to capture what EA brings in relation to acquisitions, EA needs to be understood as *a capability for orchestrating an ongoing organizational transformation across the different layers of the organization*. This capability is formed by the EA people, processes, and technology, and is enabled by the use of EA artifacts (models) that captures and conveys the output of the EA capability. At the end of the day, it does not matter what particular breed of EA framework a company uses, and neither is the state of the architecture at the beginning of a series of acquisitions of decisive importance. As a starting point, it helps if the architecture is in good condition, but what really matters is the long-term trajectory. Each transformation should improve the architecture, not create additional inefficiencies. Each minor acquisition should not bring the organization one step closer to a major organizational restructure.

Our research points to two qualities of EA capability that are particularly critical to achieve this. One is that *the EA capability must have a direct and intentional activity engagement quality*. In our work, we have often seen EA kept at arms-length from the acquisition process. EA contributes to the acquisition by providing various artifacts that map the as-is situation, but does not assume responsibilities or accountability for any tasks in the process. The EA function should be able to not only deliver input as a supplier to other organizational units, but should also actively engage in the collaborative solving of challenges with other units.

The second quality an EA should have is to be *holistic*. That is, to span across all architectural layers, from IT infrastructure and applications to operations and strategy. This might sound obvious, but because of the heritage from an era when digital technologies were only supporting business practices, most companies only use EA to orchestrate change across IT infrastructure and application layers. With the fusion of business and technology in the era of digital business, this separation is no longer effective when orchestrating acquisitions.

With these two qualities, EA can contribute to the acquisition project by (1) the *pre-acquisition preparation* of the firm to be "acquisition ready," (2) the *selection* of acquisition targets by identifying resource complementarity, (3) acquisition *integration* by directing efforts toward desirable target states, and (4) *post-integration continuation* by monitoring the achieved integration and guiding corrective action to ensure the success of the long-term growth strategy (Fig. 1.2).

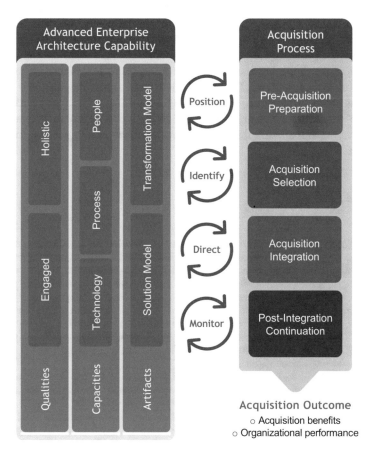

Fig. 1.2 Overview of EA contribution in the acquisition process

In this book, we go in depth into how an advanced EA capability with these two qualities can enable a value-creating acquisition process. To succeed in its value creation aspirations, the acquirer has to manage an organizational transformation across the different organizational layers in a way that leverages the synergistic potential motivating the deal, while at the same time ensuring that quick fixes, workarounds, and organizational inefficiencies do not impede future strategic moves. To this end, an advanced EA capability can help.

To explain how an advanced EA capability can be leveraged in the acquisition process, we draw on several examples that we have worked with and studied. Learning from leading companies that leverage EA in their acquisitions, we, in this book, aspire to guide the reader towards putting EA to use in acquisitions and corporate growth. We take departure in the challenge of acquisition-based growth and adopt a distinct managerial perspective with a relentless focus on how EA relates to value creation. Our ambition is to provide the reader with the cognitive keys to characterize the problem, craft effective solutions and enact these solutions.

To do this, we divide the rest of the book into three parts. In Part I we unbox the concepts of acquisitions and EA as the fundament for explaining how the two approaches combine. In Part II, we go through the different phases of an acquisition process to detail how EA can be exploited in each phase. In Part II, we provide concrete advice to managers that want to get started with putting EA to use in this novel context.

References

Accenture. (2006). *Executives report that mergers and acquisitions fail to create adequate value.* Accessed October 28, 2019, from https://newsroom.accenture.com/subjects/research-surveys/executives-report-that-mergers-and-acquisitions-fail-to-create-adequate-value.htm

Brynjolfsson, E., & McAfee, A. (2014). *The second machine age: Work, progress, and prosperity in a time of brilliant technologies.* New York, NY: WW Norton & Company.

Financial Times. (2007). *New Maersk chief makes shipping line 'top priority'.* Accessed October 28, 2019, from https://www.ft.com/content/b4de0b2e-8bdd-11dc-af4d-0000779fd2ac

Gartner. (2016). *IT primer on mergers and acquisitions.* Gartner Foundational Research, Gartner.

IMAA. (2019). *M&A statistics.* Accessed October 28, 2019, from https://imaa-institute.org/mergers-and-acquisitions-statistics/

King, D. R., Dalton, D. R., Daily, C. M., & Covin, J. G. (2004). Meta-analyses of post-acquisition performance: Indications of unidentified moderators. *Strategic Management Journal, 25*(2), 187–200.

King, D. R., McLeod, D., Samimi, M., & Cortes, A. F. (2017). A meta-analysis of 21st century acquisition research. In *Academy of Management Proceedings*, Atlanta, GA, August, 2017. Briarcliff Manor, NY: Academy of Management.

Lehn, K. M., & Zhao, M. (2006). CEO turnover after acquisitions: Are bad bidders fired? *The Journal of Finance, 61*(4), 1759–1811.

Sarrazin, H., & West, A. (2011). Understanding the strategic value of it in M&A. *McKinsey Quarterly, 12*(1), 1–6.

Part I
Framing the Issue

In Part I we will unbox the concepts of acquisitions and EA. Acquisitions are particular organizational transformations that progress through different phases and leave both short-term and long-term imprints on the merged organization. Some of these imprints are desirable, including cost and revenue synergies, while effects such as increased complexity should be avoided. Because they are organizational transformations, acquisitions are well suited to take advantage of EA practice. But to fully leverage EA in acquisitions, traditional EA capabilities are not effective. Let us take a closer look at the problem of acquisition and the proposed solution of EA.

Chapter 2
The Acquisition Challenge

Eighteen months after the acquisition of Sampo Bank for 4.1 billion euros, Danske Bank sent out a press-release announcing that "*During Easter, Danske Bank Group successfully completed the planned migration of Sampo Bank, Finland, onto the Group's IT platform.*" Completing the integration was, undeniably, an achievement. For more than a year, 2500 Danske Bank employees had been busy preparing the migration. They had carried out 50,000 tests and migrated more than two million customer accounts and 800,000 online banking agreements to Danske Bank's systems. The migration of the bank was expected to lower Sampo Bank's operational costs by 19%. Peter Straarup, chief executive of the Danske Bank Group, enthusiastically declared that "*The migration increases the competitiveness of Sampo Bank within all business areas. Our customers in Finland can now benefit from the advantages provided by a large, international bank*" (Danske Bank 2008).

However, in the time after the migration, the former Sampo Bank unit lost almost a quarter of its customers. Many different factors contributed to the drag, some had nothing to do with to the acquisition itself. For example, an untimely and possibly unrelated infrastructural breakdown at one of Danske Bank's outsourcing providers meant that Finnish customers could not use their credit cards in the days after the migration. Other contributing factors were directly related to how the two organizations were integrated. Because Danske Bank was fixated at their "One platform strategy," meaning that the whole bank should be run on one single IT platform regardless of national context, Sampo Bank's customers were migrated to Danske Bank's global IT platform, including its outdated online banking systems with only limited support for mobile banking. Pre-acquisition Sampo Bank, born and bred in the Nokia country of Finland, had one of the world's most advanced online banking solutions with a great mobile banking application. For many Sampo Bank customers, downgrading the online banking environment and the loss of possibility to use their fancy new Nokia Communicator smartphones for banking was a deal breaker, and the customers abandoned Danske Bank en masse. Danske Bank share plummeted at the Copenhagen Stock Exchange, and Sampo Bank became the last of a long stream of acquisitions by Danske Bank.

© Springer Nature Switzerland AG 2020
S. Henningsson, G. N. Toppenberg, *Architecting Growth in the Digital Era*,
https://doi.org/10.1007/978-3-030-39482-0_2

This story of Danske Bank and Sampo Bank could have ended then and there, as a warning example of how difficult it is to substantiate acquisition benefits. But this is a story of the many nuances of these acts. One of the reasons Danske Bank stuck firmly to its one-platform strategy was because it facilitated innovation. Having a single platform allowed the bank to "build once and deploy everywhere," instead of redeveloping new product and process innovations in every country where the bank was present. With increasing digitalization of finance, and the turning of banking into a digital innovation arms race, the single platform strategy has proven vital for rapid innovation and something that sets Danske Bank apart from its competitors. Enabled by the single platform-strategy, Danske Bank is today one of the most innovative actors in the financial industry, as evidenced by its success in smartphone apps for banking services. The bank's Mobilepay app is today installed on 9 out of 10 smartphones in Denmark and has become the de facto standard for mobile payments in the country. This innovativeness would not had been possible if they had abandoned their one-platform strategy to accommodate the specific online banking environment of Sampo Bank. So, the damage done to Sampo Bank was not without a good long-term rationale.

We do not say that long-term objectives should overshadow short-term benefits. Without short-term gains there is no long-term future. But what the story of Danske Bank and Sampo Bank illustrates is the complexity of the acquisition challenge and the many ways to think about relevant acquisition outcomes. Therefore, before we go into the workings of EA and how an advanced EA capability can be leveraged in acquisitions, we need to decompose the acquisition challenge into its constituents. We do so in three steps that match the three core issues in an acquisition challenge (Fig. 2.1). First, we discuss the different value creating reasons that make firms engage in acquisitions. We then turn to the multiple layers of relevant outcomes on which acquisition success can be judged. Finally, we present a generic process model that described the activities linking acquisition outset to outcomes. This process model is later used as a fundament to discuss the specific role EA can serve in each phase of the model.

Acquisition Types

Acquisitions take place for many reasons and in many different forms. Some acquisitions may in a legal sense be mergers, or communicated as mergers to not scare off the individuals working in the acquired business. Our broad definition of acquisition is an organizational consolidation where there is one dominating who can drive and make decisions about the acquisition and integration work to be done.

Acquisitions can be of complete, stand-alone businesses or specific business units that are divested by one company and acquired by another. These two acts have much in common, but also some fundamental distinctions. They have in common that they are motivated by the basic idea that the two combined units are better off together than independently. This "better off" refers to the synergies that can be

Fig. 2.1 Core issues of an acquisition challenge

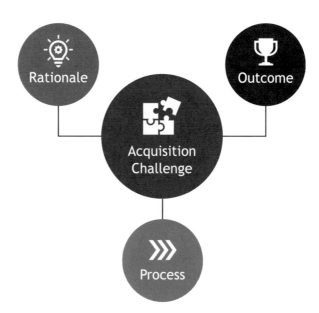

created post-acquisition. Synergies are created by a set of value-creating mechanisms that are common of both complete business and divestment acquisitions.

The difference between the two types of acquisitions are that complete business acquisitions would normally come with all IT resources needed to retain the business status quo. Creating synergies, the acquiring organization has full degrees of freedom when devising the integration plan. In contrast, in a divestment to acquisition transaction, the business unit will lose its previous parent organization. With this, typically also some of its IT enablement. It follows that options to move are constrained and time pressure for completion is increased as the integration project must be finished before expensive transition contracts overshadow any synergistic value. This notable difference is most salient in the integration project as the acquisition integration project needs to be harmonized with the divestment project.

The value-creating motivations can be sorted into four broad acquisition categories: Deepening, Extending, Enhancing, and Renewal acquisitions (Henningsson et al. 2018). These four categories of acquisitions create value in distinct ways and require different post-acquisition integration strategies to substantiate the value (see Table 2.1).

Deepening One of the principle reasons to acquire is to further exploit an already successful business strategy. For Danske Bank, economies of scale were one of the main reasons to acquire other European banks. The cost structure for operating and developing the IT systems required for a complete retail bank are characterized by a large fixed cost and a low marginal cost. That meant that the cost of IT was relatively stable regardless of how many customers the bank had. With more customers, the bank's cost per customer would be lowered and make the bank more competitive.

Table 2.1 Acquisition motivation and integration strategies

Acquisition type	Acquisition motivation	Integration approach	Technological enablement
Deepening	Economies of scale	Absorption	Migration
Extending	Economies of scope	Preservation	Coexistence
Enhancing	Business improvement	Symbiosis	Best-of-breed
Renewing	Strategic repositioning	Redesign	Redevelopment

Another firm that has made business-deepening acquisitions to a core corporate strategy is the Mexican cement manufacturer CEMEX (Ross et al. 2006). Through a global acquisition program, CEMEX has become the world's largest cement manufacturer benefiting from economies of scale and low production costs in an industry characterized by low degrees of differentiation in the offering.

CEMEX integrates its acquisitions with an integration strategy of absorption. The acquired firm is decomposed and assimilated into CEMEX's structures and business processes. In cement manufacturing, there is little need for local variations so CEMEX can utilize the very same business capabilities almost everywhere in the world. Technology wise, the acquired business is migrated to CEMEX's preexisting technological capabilities and generally no exceptions are made from the standard system templates.

Extending A second rational to acquire is the extension of existing business to include new offerings. Business-extending acquisitions produce value through economies of scope—the simultaneous delivering of two different offerings to their market is more effective than independently. Economies of scope can come from shared production, distribution, marketing, and sales activities.

When DuPont, a US-based conglomerate with business in various chemical industries, acquired Danish food ingredients company Danisco, the main rationale behind the acquisition was expected economies of scope (Henningsson 2016). Because Danisco's customers largely overlap with the customers of DuPont, the firm expected that Danisco's customers could be more efficiently served if Danisco became a part of the DuPont conglomerate.

To integrate Danisco, DuPont used a partial preservation strategy. For the areas where economies of scope where to be expected, Danisco's business capabilities were absorbed into DuPont's business capabilities. This included distribution and sales, for example. In other areas, Danisco functioned quite differently, and in order to preserve the competitiveness of Danisco, these areas were left intact. Technologically, Danisco was integrated with a partial coexistence approach, meaning that in overlapping areas Danisco was migrated to DuPont's enabling technological capabilities while in its unique areas Danisco retained its unique technological capabilities.

Enhancing A third subgroup of acquisitions is aimed at accessing innovative technologies and related capabilities required to exploit these technologies in the market place, and is commonly referred to as technology acquisitions. Technology acquisitions take place in any industry that competes on product or process innovation, including construction, pharmaceutical and chemicals, but are generally most commonly seen in high-tech industries and in particular in industries based on digital technologies. Companies such as Cisco, Apple, Google, Facebook and Amazon all complete a double-digit number of acquisitions every year just to keep up with the innovation phase in their respective markets. Today, however, we are starting to see the same numbers of digital technology acquisitions in industries that traditionally are not seen as digital, such as finance and automotive. Between 2012 and 2015, acquisitions in Auto Tech grew by 40%. Specifically, acquisitions related to embedded software and hardware grew between 2014 and 2015 with 244% in volume (Hampleton Partners 2016).

For SAP SE, the German enterprise software firm, technology acquisitions are an indispensable means to survive technology transitions in the industry (Dowie et al. 2017). Since the inception of the company, the delivery of enterprise software has evolved from mainframes to client-server architecture, and most recently towards on-demand software service. In 2005, SAP started to realize that it needed to innovate to support a client base that was transitioning to a digital world. Following its traditional and proven approach, SAP initially tried to do so through internal innovation. However, SAP's established (e.g., Oracle) and emerging (e.g., salesforce.com) competitors were able to quickly and significantly increase their market shares in the area of cloud software and other competitive spaces. Consequently, SAP's executives decided on an acquisition program to fuel the transition. This strategic shift resulted in a multitude of smaller and a number of larger acquisitions. For example, SAP acquired the business intelligence company Business Objects in 2008 and the database company Sybase in 2010.

The challenge of technology acquisitions is to find a symbiosis model where the strengths of both companies are combined. SAP recognizes that the acquired unit may be better performing in its expertise area than SAP itself. For example, when SAP acquired Hybris for its innovative solutions for omni-channel sales, SAP wanted to integrate Hybris in a way that enabled exploitation of these innovative solutions together with SAP extant offerings and business models. Integrating Hybris through absorption would potentially destroy the innovative business capabilities for which SAP acquired Hybris. Integrating Hybris with a coexistence strategy would retain Hybris's innovativeness, but make impossible any further exploitation within an SAP context. Therefore, a joint governance structure with representatives from both SAP and Hybris was set up to carefully blend the business practices in a way that did not destroy the innovative edge of Hybris. Gradually, SAP's preexisting e-commerce business unit was moved to Hybris, which over 3 years following the acquisition grew from 800 to 3000 employees.

Technologically, Hybris was integrated with a best-of-breed approach. This meant that the combining companies selectively investigate the technological enablement of the practices to make sure that "shoehorning" Hybris's business capabilities into SAP's enabling technological capabilities did not harm the way to do business. When needed and possible, Hybris's enabling technologies were retained as new standards for omni-channel software development. The exception was where Hybris's pre-acquisition used software from SAP's competitors. In these special cases, SAP's enabling technological capabilities were reconfigured to meet the ways Hybris was working.

Renewing Acquisitions can also be used to induce strategic renewal in firms that have stagnated or for other reasons are in need for strategic repositioning. It is widely accepted that companies such as the camera producer Kodak, the mobile phone company Nokia, and the typewriter manufacture Smith Corona were disrupted because they did not spot the digital trends in their respective industries. The reality is, however, slightly different. Kodak was itself the inventor of the digital camera. In 1996, Nokia released the first smartphone more than a decade before Apple released the iPhone. Smith Corona was a frontrunner in word processing typewriters with its PWP 1400 model. So, the issue that brought these companies down was not that they were unable to see the technological trends. The issue was that they could not reinvent themselves to be relevant as their respective industries transformed. Large, more mature firms typically have difficulties transforming and adopting radically to new ways of working because of their norms, values, competences, reward systems, and other characteristics that are adapted to the business model that has made the firm successful in the past. To overcome such rigidities, firms attempt to induce strategic renewal by inducing means required through acquisitions.

Acquisitions rarely lead to complete renewals of the whole acquiring firms, but can be made to reposition specific strategic business units. This was the case when the international industry group Trelleborg acquired the French firm Kléber to reposition its industrial hose business (Henningsson and Carlsson 2011). Before the acquisition, Trelleborg's industrial hose business was a small niche player competing unsuccessfully for a niche position in the premium-quality hose market. The business and technological capabilities of the unit was tailored to support the niche strategy. Through the acquisition of Kléber, Trelleborg acquired the production capacities and market share to reposition the hose business as a low-cost, market leading industrial hose manufacturer.

Because of the new business strategy, Trelleborg needed to integrate Kléber following an organizational redesign strategy. Trelleborg completely redrew the organizational chart of its hose business, made national companies into sales offices, centralized distribution networks, and consolidated production capacities. To technically support the new organization, Trelleborg retired all the technical capabilities that were tailored to support the former niche strategy and implemented new central, low-cost capabilities to support the new low-cost business strategy. The complete transformation of all business and technology capabilities took 10 years to implement. While such strategic renewals are typically considered high-risk and long-term games, Trelleborg's acquisition of Kléber illustrates that strategic renewal acquisitions can also create value if appropriately executed.

It should be recognized that while smaller acquisitions can be made with a single acquisition objective in mind, most large acquisitions will involve a mix of different acquisition benefits. For example, in the Sampo Bank acquisition, Danske Bank had the opportunity to deepen the business and create economies of scale through its single IT platform, but also the opportunity for business enhancement through technological innovation in online banking if the bank would have been able to build scale while at the same time preserve and exploit Sampo Bank's state-of-the-art mobile banking capabilities. Multiple acquisition objectives increase the necessity for EA best practice. The challenges of managing the separate work streams required for multiple acquisition objectives are further discussed in relation to the acquisition process below.

Acquisition Outcomes

Acquisitions are notoriously difficult to judge as successful or not, because we never have a reference scenario for what would have happened if the acquisition had not taken place. An acquisition may lead a company to a dire state, but things could have been even worse without the acquisition. Conversely, a company may be performing well despite its latest stream of struggling acquisitions.

Yet, being able to discuss acquisition performance is of utmost important for managing acquisitions towards value creation. For such a discussion, it is critical to understand that outcomes take place on different levels that may be correlated, but may also be mutually excluding and involve explicit trade-offs. Using the example of Danske Bank acquiring Sampo Bank, we can differentiate between the outcomes directly related to the short-term acquisition benefits and the outcomes related to long-term organizational performance (see Table 2.2 for an overview).

Short-term acquisition performance includes integration efficiency and the effectiveness of the acquisition to substantiate possible business benefits. In the Sampo Bank acquisition, the integration efficiency and acquisition effectiveness outcomes were in direct opposition. Danske Bank estimated that every month of delay in the integration would cost approximately USD $30 million in missed operational synergies and resource consumption. While integrated, Sampo Bank was expected to have 19% lower operational costs. Therefore, the bank felt a strong need to push forwards with the integration despite the awareness that for Sampo Bank customers,

Table 2.2 Acquisition performance

Time horizon	Performance category	Description
Short-term acquisition benefits	Acquisition efficiency	Time and cost for executing the acquisition
	Acquisition effectiveness	Business benefits generated through acquisition
Long-term organizational performance	Sustained growth	Possibilities to continue acquisition-based growth
	Exploitation opportunities	The ability to seize future strategic options

the online banking experience would mean a step backwards. To Sampo Bank customers, it was communicated that the downgrade would only be temporary, and once the migration was completed the additional resources available would be used to further develop the merged bank. However, as history tells us, Sampo Bank customers were not satisfied with the promise and abandoned the bank. In that sense, although integration was highly efficient, the acquisition was not effective in generating all the possible benefits of deepening and enhancing the business.

In the Sampo Bank case, the retrospective wisdom is that it would probably have been better to push the migration 6–12 months, to first rebuild Sampo Bank's online banking solution on Danske Bank's platform before making the migration. The destructive effects on acquisition value of prioritizing integration efficiency may be comparatively small. Yet in other cases, delay may not even be an option. This was the case for Commonwealth Bank of Australia, when it acquired State Bank of Victoria (Johnston and Yetton 1996). After having struggled with delays caused by the technological best-of-breed integration that would enable a selective symbiosis strategy to exploit some of State Bank of Victoria's superior business capabilities, legal authorities demanded that integration should be executed rapidly so that the bank could commence joint financial reporting and risk management. At this stage, the Commonwealth Bank of Australia saw no other option than to execute integration with a full absorption approach and full technological migration.

The outcome of acquisitions also has to be understood in terms of its *long-term impact on organizational performance*, specifically the possibility to exploit future growth options. Such future growth options can include subsequent acquisitions. Most acquisitions are not isolated events, but are part of strategic growth programs that completely or partly rely on sets of acquisitions. Serial acquirers, defined as making at least two acquisitions every 3 years, make 60% of all acquisitions (Kengelbach et al. 2011). So, frequently, an acquisition is only one component in a sequence of related acquisitions to implement a corporate growth-by-acquisition strategy.

In acquisition programs, the performance of one acquisition must be understood in relation to previous and future acquisitions. For example, an integration project under severe time pressure to realize acquisition benefits adopts ad hoc solutions that, in the short term, deliver direct acquisition benefits. However, at the same time, those solutions compromise the long-term viability of the organization's technological platform. In a growth-by-acquisition program, this effect could significantly reduce the acquirer's flexibility, limiting its capacity to support technology-enabled strategic innovations elsewhere in the organization.

Empirical evidence shows that after an initial round of acquisitions, serial acquirers frequently put their acquisition programs on hold to undertake a major organizational restructuration. This is because the initial integration challenges are solved suboptimally, resulting in organizational inefficiencies. Cumulatively, these inefficiencies threaten the viability of the acquisition program. When the level of organizational inefficiency reaches a critical level, a major organizational transformation program is launched. Although it will typically be financially unjustifiable to engage in such major organizational change for each individual acquisition undertaken, the potential benefits of doing so may often become very real after a firm has undertaken a string of acquisitions over time (Barkema and Schijven 2008).

CEMEX, well known for its efficient integration routine to effectuate business deepening acquisitions, launched a major platform project in 2010. The justification was that *"The complexity of integrating many acquisitions in the late 2000s were impeding CEMEX's continued growth"* (Villate and Little 2011). The Harvard case library contains many other examples of cases where a sequence of acquisitions have forced the acquirer to undertake a major IT platform project. These include iAutomation, Aux Bons Soins, and Bombardier.

Returning to the Sampo Bank acquisition, one possible integration scenario would have been for Danske Bank to abandon its one-platform strategy and integrate Sampo Bank's online banking solution as a redundant technological capability alongside Danske Bank's existing corresponding capability. However, this design was rejected because it would make the platform more complex and less efficient. It would not support well a continued acquisition-based growth and, more importantly, not allow for efficient innovation post-acquisition. While the effects of one single exception would have been relatively small, Danske Bank held firmly to its one-platform strategy because it knew of the importance of retaining platform consistency in order to compete on innovation.

The Acquisition Process

The execution of an acquisition proceeds through four interdependent phases (Fig. 2.2) (Yetton et al. 2013). First, the acquisition process starts well before a potential target has been identified by making the acquirer "ready to acquire." *Pre-acquisition preparation* takes place over a period of time that is measured in years. During this period, management builds the resources needed, including a flexible IT platform that can accommodate new businesses to manage acquisitions and develops top management's trust in those resources.

When Danske Bank acquired Sampo Bank, Danske Bank's possibility to acquire Sampo Bank was conditioned on how a number of events were handled in the years leading up to the acquisition. Importantly, the single-platform strategy was decided already in the late 1980s when Danske Bank was formed through a three-way merger and decided to take the platform consolidation work in order to have a single platform ready for future growth. Then, following a series of acquisitions across Europe, Danske Bank held firmly to its strategy in order not to compromise future growth.

Second, the acquirer must select the right target to acquire. The *selection* phase comprises the identification of threats from and opportunities for post-acquisition resource combinations, and an estimate of their potential value. Frequently, acquisitions are motivated by a number of different business benefits that together are assumed to exceed the premium paid by the acquirer for control over the target. This

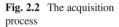 **Fig. 2.2** The acquisition process

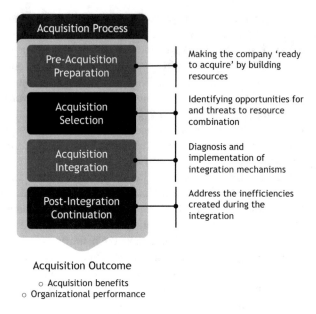

requires a deep understanding of the acquirer's own resources, as well as the ability to assess the acquisition's stock of resources. A particular source of value comes from the parenting of strategic business units. This means that one large corporation may choose to divest a particular business unit to an acquiring company because the acquirer has what is called a parenting advantage.

The selection of Sampo Bank involved a careful analysis of all possible benefits of the acquisition, including the primary benefits of scale in operation but also secondary benefits in terms of new products that could render economies of scope and innovative technologies, such as the online banking solution. The selection entailed matching all Sampo Bank capabilities with what currently existed in Danske Bank to understand similarities and differences. Selection also included an assessment of the extent the different benefits could be substantiated, which resulted in the conclusion that the primary benefits of scale would be achievable, whereas benefits of scope and technological innovation would be more difficult to realize.

Third, the acquirer must *integrate* the target. This entails diagnosis and implementation of the integration mechanisms to realize the benefits of scale, scope, resource addition, and strategic renewal, which are all dependent on different integration mechanisms. In addition, the acquirer must limit the integration's potentially negative impact on the acquirer's overall performance. Frequently, acquisition integration is solved suboptimally, introducing organizational inefficiencies, such as increased complexity, and reduced business and IT alignment. Suboptimal solutions may be necessary in the short term, but will, if not corrected, have a long-term negative impact on the acquirer.

Acquisitions of carved-out divestments could be particularly difficult to integrate because they would typically come with a complete IT enablement as a start. This gives a hard deadline for the integration project that is also contingent on the activities of the vendor. If the vendor gets delayed, this will spill over on the acquirer. Or even worse, if the vendor cannot manage to decouple IT enablement from the vendor's remaining business, there might be critical gaps in the enablement. This would further add to the integration challenge.

In Danske Bank's acquisition of Sampo, integration was solved suboptimally because not all acquisition benefits were materialized. This would have required a more complex integration with several different work streams focusing on the distinct benefits. On the other hand, Danske Bank managed to keep the long-term viability of the company by not making short-sighted solutions to the enabling technological capabilities.

Fourth, in *post-integration continuation*, the acquirer must address the organizational inefficiencies created during the integration. Achieving acquisition benefits without compromising long-term firm performance is of particular importance for the many "serial acquirers" that make several acquisitions per year, as inefficiencies would rapidly accumulate, threatening the firms' growth strategies.

Specifically, in Danske Bank's acquisition of Sampo Bank, the post-integration continuation phase implied rebuilding of the capabilities that had been destroyed in the acquisition, for example, the online banking solution. Using the efficiency improvements to fuel new development made it possible to boost innovation and regain lost market share. Post-integration continuation also meant addressing the IT infrastructure robustness that was suffering from the many time-constraint modifications that had been pushed out over the years and now was making the infrastructure highly unstable.

Within this generic acquisition process, a specific acquisition can take various paths depending on the value-creating rationale of acquisition. Therefore, depending on the outcome of one phase, the activities in the next phase are frequently very different. For example, if in the selection phase an opportunity for an absorption acquisition is identified, the integration of such acquisition will require fundamentally different tasks to be completed, compared to when an opportunity for a symbiosis acquisition is identified. In a preservation acquisition, very little integration work will be required. However, most large acquisitions present a number of distinct acquisition benefits, and therefore progress through the phases of the acquisition process through parallel work streams seeking to leverage each benefit. To manage this complex organizational transformation, an advanced EA capability can help.

Chapter Key Points

- Acquisitions are made for many different reasons, including scale, scope, business improvement, and strategic repositioning.

- Each acquisition objective is leveraged by a different integration mechanism; in a large acquisition with several objectives, one needs to combine integration mechanisms.
- Short-term acquisition outcomes include acquisition efficiency (time, budget) and acquisition effectiveness (synergies).
- Long-term implications include effects on future growth possibilities and impact on overall profit.
- The four key phases of an acquisition project are: preparation, selection, integration, and continuation.

References

Barkema, H. G., & Schijven, M. (2008). Toward unlocking the full potential of acquisitions: The role of organizational restructuring. *Academy of Management Journal, 51*(4), 696–722.

Danske Bank. (2008). *Sampo Bank on Danske BankGroup's platform*. Company Announcement No. 12/2008.

Dowie, J., Henningsson, S., Kude, T., & Popp. K. (2017). Merging platform ecosystems in technology acquisitions: A governance perspective. In: *The 25th European Conference on Information Systems (ECIS)* (pp. 2301–2316). Association for Information Systems, AIS Electronic Library (AISeL).

Hampleton Partners. (2016). *Automotive Technology M&A 2015*. Hampleton Partners: Autotech M&A Report.

Henningsson, S. (2016). The acquisition IT integration challenge: Danisco/DuPont. In N. B. Andersen (Ed.), *Cases on IT leadership* (pp. 123–142). Samfundslitteratur: Copenhagen.

Henningsson, S., & Carlsson, S. (2011). The DySIIM model for managing IS integration in mergers and acquisitions. *Information Systems Journal, 21*(5), 441–476.

Henningsson, S., Yetton, P. W., & Wynne, P. J. (2018). A review of information system integration in mergers and acquisitions. *Journal of Information Technology, 33*(4), 255–303.

Johnston, K. D., & Yetton, P. W. (1996). Integrating information technology divisions in a bank merger fit, compatibility and models of change. *The Journal of Strategic Information Systems, 5* (3), 189–211.

Kengelbach, J., Klemmer, D., Schwetzler, B., Sperling, M., & Roos, A. (2011). *Does practice make perfect? How the top serial acquirers create value*. Boston: Boston Consulting Group.

Ross, J. W., Weill, P., & Robertson, D. (2006). *Enterprise architecture as strategy: Creating a foundation for business execution*. Boston, MA: Harvard Business Press.

Villate, R., & Little, G. (2011). *CEMEX process and IT transformation: Delivering value through an integrated business process model*. IDC Case Study. IDC.

Yetton, P., Henningsson, S., & Bjorn-Andersen, N. (2013). Ready to acquire': IT resources for a growth-by-acquisition strategy. *MIS Quarterly Executive, 12*(1), 19–35.

Chapter 3
The Advanced Enterprise Architecture Capability

The pace of change in today's business world is dramatic. In an effort to remain relevant, businesses continue to be challenged to renew their competitive advantage. Examples of constant change can be seen across industries where the reality for the majority of companies is the choice to adapt or perish—a choice to evolve beyond current offerings, markets, and customers and a choice to transform and potentially disrupt the status quo. EA has a unique opportunity to aid companies looking to gain a competitive advantage through its methods and principles of helping to organize, structure, and lead transformational efforts, but leaders will need to rethink the specific role EA teams can play, moving them from traditional documentation activities to advanced planning and execution activities.

The J.M. Smucker Company, a consumer packaged goods company based in the USA is one such enterprise that has had to rethink how it utilizes EA in a much more progressive way throughout the company to enable organizational transformations, including acquisitions (Bhogill and Covington 2011). Fueled by acquisitive growth, Smucker grew from a $500 million company to a $5 billion company in just 10 years. The J.M. Smucker Company became one of the fastest growing companies in the consumer packaged goods industry. Its family of brands included Smucker's®, Folgers®, Jif®, Crisco®, Pillsbury®, Eagle Brand®, R.W. Knudsen Family®, Hungry Jack®, and many more.

As Smucker continued to expand its portfolio of leading brands, the company needed to devise a practice that could enable it to cope with the continuously more complex ongoing transformation. Focusing on not only the technology integration challenges but instead coordination and integration throughout the company, Smucker's EA discipline helped the organization avoid some of the most common and costly mistakes that often plague companies. At Smucker, the engagement of EA started already in the formulation of strategy, where capability maps are used to expose gaps in the existing portfolio and to discuss how strategic opportunities relates to current businesses. EA furthermore used an EA framework that helped them resolve how strategic visions should be translated into operational practice. They engaged the EA function not only for the information and application tiers,

© Springer Nature Switzerland AG 2020

S. Henningsson, G. N. Toppenberg, *Architecting Growth in the Digital Era*,
https://doi.org/10.1007/978-3-030-39482-0_3

which are what we would consider traditional EA areas of focus but also in the business tier. At this tier, the EA strategy helped align with the organization's operating model, strategy, and objectives, guiding transformations by providing a business-centric view of the enterprise from a functional perspective. In addition to being business centric, the EA team was also considering the usability of their artifacts and recommendation in the execution of the acquisition integration; they transitioned to focusing on the process of architecting and away from purely developing architectures. EA also evolved into a standard feature of project management with virtual EA teams meeting every week to discuss how architectural thinking could assist the ongoing transformations. This ensured that the EA team was continually engaged in the delivery of their recommendations and can guide the execution as needed.

The advanced EA capability of Smucker is in strong contrast to many traditional EA capabilities. EA has a historical past closely related to the technical disciplines. With roots that can be traced back to the business systems planning initiated by IBM in the 1960s, the first EA frameworks started to appear in the 1980s. From the 1990s and onwards, relatively modern frameworks such as FEAF[1] and TOGAF[2] were introduced as extensions of some of the previous practices. This means that even today, many traditional EA practices are formed upon the seminal ideas that trace back to the business systems planning approach of the 1960s. These ideas commonly include a focus on technology and systems architecture, a top-down architecture planning approach, a formal step-wise architecture planning process, and various diagrams and matrices for describing the architecture.

The consequence of its legacy is that EA has taken on a poor reputation, attributed as "ivory tower" and "in the clouds," focused only on documentation and strategic speculation, while developing artifacts that may or may not be used. This type of EA practice is a rigid, expensive, and time-consuming planning exercise that renders abstract plans that are difficult to understand and implement. As EA activities commonly take place in isolation from the rest of the organization, EA documentation is typically ignored in strategic decision-making and the technical architectures produced are "useful as little more than doorstops" (Ross et al. 2006, p. vii).

But advanced EA practices such as the one at Smucker have been able to break free of the historical heritage to become essential enablers of strategy in the digital economy. What makes them different? It is not the EA frameworks they adopt or the techniques employed for updating EA artifacts, such as reference models and roadmaps. Sure, the right set of tools help, but it's not where difference is created. Instead, the advanced EA capability is defined by how EA people, processes, and technology enable the leveraging of EA artifacts. The right composition of people, processes, and technology give the advanced EA capability two distinct qualities: the *holistic* and the *engaged* quality. In Fig. 3.1 the purposes, qualities, capacities, and

---

[1]Federal Enterprise Architecture (FEA). https://obamawhitehouse.archives.gov/omb/e-gov/FEA

[2]The TOGAF® Standard. http://www.opengroup.org/subjectareas/enterprise/togaf

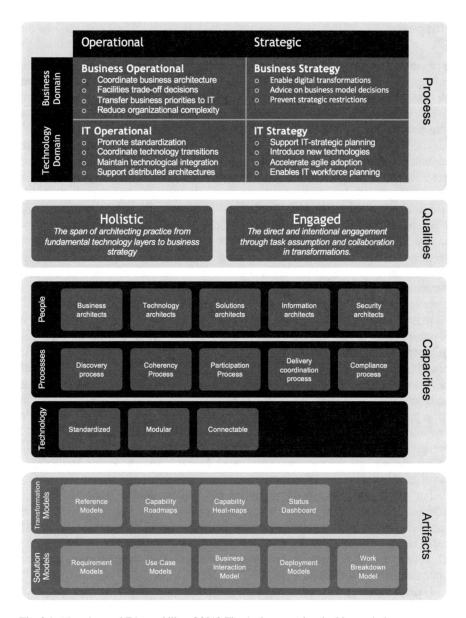

Fig. 3.1 The advanced EA capability. ©2019 The Authors, reprinted with permission

artifacts of an advanced EA capability are outlined. In the following, these constituents are presented in detail.

Purposes

The gradual transition of EA from a traditional capability with focus on technology management, to an advanced capability that contributes to the business strategy can be described as a journey along two dimensions. On one hand, EA has transformed from a technology focus to include a business focus. At the same time, EA has also transformed from operational management to be embraced in strategy formulation.

The traditional IT operational EA purposes include tasks associated with maintaining an efficient technological infrastructure that becomes an asset to and not a liability for organizational performance. This includes specific purposes such as the promotion of technology standards across the organization and the maintaining of technological consistency to avoid disruption in technology enablement. The IT operational role of EA also includes facilitation of the techno- logical integration of the organization, for example, through the promotion of service-oriented architecture (SOA) and other architectural principles, or the support of distributed technology architecture. In the IT-operational role, EA should also coordinate technology transitions so that they take place in the most efficient order and avoid redundant work.

In the IT-strategic role, EA purposes pertain to proactive objectives that are aimed at not only maintaining status quo, but also suggest how the IT function should better meet organizational demands in the future. This includes the support of strategic planning to create an effective IT strategy and to contribute to the introduction of new technologies both by identifying them, but also by ensuring that they can be embraced when identified. Within the IT-strategic role, EA also holds some keys to the espousal of Agile adoption in that EA have significant opportunities to help Agile projects move more quickly and be more effective. Furthermore, EA has a purpose to serve in IT workforce planning in that it should have a comprehensive understanding of the current and future competence need in the IT function, and the balance between the two.

For organizations that have expanded the EA function to comprise also the business levels of the organization, the business-operational EA purposes relate to the maintaining of an effective and streamlined organization without undesired redundancies. In this role, EA also has the purpose to position the business as the IT customer, which includes the transfer of user experience between business operations and IT functions.

Finally, for the most advanced EA capabilities, the business strategic purposes connect with active contribution to expanding the business potential. This includes preventing IT from restraining directions in which the business strategy might evolve. EA can also contribute to the development of business models through its insights into how business capabilities are technologically enabled. Ultimately, EA has a critical purpose in orchestrating complete organizational transformation across all organizational levels to exploit the opportunities presented by digitalization.

Qualities

In organizations where EA still assumes a traditional role, the important qualities of the EA function includes characteristics such as thorough, detailed, and timely. But these qualities are part of what has made EA widely criticized for being an expensive documentation exercise. For EA being able to fulfill its more advanced purposes, an EA function with other qualities is needed.

The Holistic Quality

To explain how EA can form part of business strategy making, it is necessary to start with how strategy is developed. Much has been written about the strategies that companies employ to evolve and transform themselves, evoking the image of a new path moving forward that takes them from industry laggard to new market, customers, and opportunities. In most organizations, an institutional strategy followed by the development of strategic initiatives or programs to realize the strategies is formulated in direct response to an opportunity in the business environment. Strategic intent at the top is usually the initial catalyst for change and transformation and involves the identification of an opportunity to exploit or the pressure to turn around a failing business.

Whatever the catalyst for the change, the process typically starts from the top. It is not surprising that when Forbes asked CEOs of the top 500 companies (LSA Global 2019) they said that they believed their companies did a good job of articulating a strategy to remain competitive (82%). The same group was, however, significantly less sure that they were able to execute the strategies and realize outcomes (14%). Given their response, it is surprising that much less attention has been spent on the process of managing change or transformation than the process of connecting strategic intent with the ability to execute a vision.

For enterprises, translating strategies into outcomes is an issue that causes well-positioned companies not to transform in a way that is beneficial to their ongoing survival and growth. The challenge for many senior leaders who decide on the strategic initiatives and vision for the enterprise is the inability to determine an effective way to translate that strategy into a useful roadmap for execution teams to follow. We believe that it would be unwise to undertake a major transformation in an enterprise without forethought and that the role of EA has a vital role to play in ensuring transformation initiatives are carefully planned and executed against a blueprint with a current and target state.

Looking back at the example of Smucker, EA has become a key player in translating strategic visions into outcomes. Similar to many other organizations, EA started as a technological practice, but has evolved to a practice with a focus on aligning all levels of the organization: from strategy to operation, systems, and infrastructure technology. The starting point in the architectural thinking is a

Fig. 3.2 The role of EA—connecting strategy and execution

business-centric view of the enterprise, and subsequent levels of architecture depict the capabilities that enable business strategies. In any given transformation, be it an acquisition or another type of organizational transformation, the changes required to enable the strategic vision are worked into the always updated roadmaps for each architectural level. For the leadership team at Smucker, having future-state architecture artifacts allows them to be proactive in the critical situations that arise and make acute decisions based on the architecture artifacts the EA team has produced.

What EA at Smucker has is the holistic quality of connecting across all organizational layers, with architects both in basic business and technical functions such as IT, allowing for company executives to develop strategies and then establish an architectural linkage to the current and future state of the organization. Here the execution teams find benefit from understanding where their projects play a role in enabling the desired business transformation and the migration from a current to a target state. The connected benefit that EA plays between strategy and execution can be seen in Fig. 3.2.

The Engaged Quality

EA at Smucker also presented a second defining quality in that it is *engaged*. The traditional mode of engagement of EA is indirect. In this mode, EA engaged through the provision of models and other artifacts that were then used in the organizational processes, such as transformations. For example, EA provides an enterprise reference model upon request that is used in understanding existing capabilities to enter a related market. The indirect mode represents an "output-input" relation between EA and the rest of the organization, where EA is kept at arms-length—or, if you will, in its ivory tower.

The indirect engagement mode continues to be relevant, as there are certain situations where EA serves its purposes by simply delivering reference material or work in predefined plans in the ongoing transformation. However, to fully effectuate all purposes of the advanced EA capability, a second engagement mode is required: the direct mode. Direct engagement refers to the specific tasks the EA team is engaged in to perform tasks in specific organizational projects, forming an integrated constituent of the organizational capability in question. In direct engagement, EA assumes tasks in a project because it is considered the best-positioned group to perform the task. For example, instead of delivering the capability models that are used by business development to investigate if the company has the capabilities to move into a related market, EA is assigned to perform the investigation task because EA can best understand what relevant capabilities the company currently possesses and what will be required to operate in the new market.

This difference between indirect and direct engagement is simple but fundamental, because if EA assumes the task, EA can actively contribute to shaping the business strategy, for example, by suggesting that extant capabilities can, with relative ease, be extended to operate the new market in one way, while another business model would require fundamentally different operational and technological capabilities.

Capacities

Examining the two critical qualities of an advanced EA capability reveals that both the *holistic* and the *engagement* qualities are produced by a set of capacities that are very different from what is typically included in a traditional EA capability.

Regarding the engagement quality, the indirect engagement corresponds well with the description use of EA. The description use, relative to the design and evaluation use, represents a relatively basic use of EA. The direct engagement corresponds well with the design and evaluation use of EA. To achieve this, the EA team needs a profound understanding of not only the technical aspect of EA, but also of the business strategic objectives that the firm seeks to achieve. Without such understanding, the EA team cannot be given the responsibility to complete tasks such as investigating the potential of strategic moves, to-be state definition, and progression analysis.

People

The relevant people in the EA function are architects. Figure 3.1 presents some of the more common architectural roles in an advanced EA capability. In some settings, not all roles are applicable. Security architects, for example, may be too ambitious at some places with low security requirements. In other settings, additional architectural roles will be required. The fundamental argument behind the list of roles presented in Fig. 3.1 is, however, that the architectural roles should span areas that match the two critical qualities of an advanced EA capability.

To enable the holistic quality, it is natural that the EA function comprises both business and technology architects. Business architects typically work with the business strategy and operational layers of the organizations. Typically, they document program and project portfolios, business processes, and employee roles.

While some think of technology architects as purely working with infrastructural technologies, we see technology architects covering both the systems and infrastructural layers of the organization. In their capacities they work with IT services, information systems, networks, databases, and other infrastructural components. Sometimes technology architects also denote architects working with data elements, such as business objects, data entities, and data quality, while others denote this as a specific architectural role of the information architect.

Solutions architects are relevant at several levels, some can work on the enterprise level in defining to-be scenarios and future states in a business initiative, while others work on the project level to ensure that the transformation implemented adheres to good architectural principles.

Processes

To use EA is all about activity. An EA capability performs an ongoing process of discovery for an organization about how it relates to its future business, operations, systems, and technology. A specific EA model is always an incomplete representation of the company. It is as correct as needed in the critical areas, and available as required. The emphasis is on "architecting" rather than "architecture." This differs from the more traditional view of EA as a complete and accurate representation of a company.

This process of ongoing discovery we refer to as the *discovery process*. The EA discovery process defines sequences of activities that are required in order to develop the EA framework and its contents. Both the target state EA blueprint and the current state EA blueprint are developed in iterations in a "just in time" basis. It's simply too expensive and too complex to maintain correct, detailed models of all areas at any time. Instead, models should be as correct as needed.

The *coherency process* is the process of managing EA as a whole created from its parts. That is, the EA coherency analyzes capabilities at all organizational layers, business, operational, systems, and technology capabilities, and how they together form a whole: the enterprise. This analysis entails identifying pain points at the different levels and inconsistencies in the enablement of business capabilities. When inconsistencies exist, EA should initiate corrective action. The process also includes a proactive stance in the definition of standards and guidelines to ensure future coherency.

The *participation process* refers to how EA interacts with other functions to identify and disseminate information in a timely manner. The participation process takes place at two levels. At a general level, architecture principles, policies, decisions, recommendations, deliverables, contracts, and agreements are proactively communicated. On the project level, EA should be included early to ensure that the projects are driven by an architectural mindset that seizes opportunities in the current state and evolves as a coherent whole.

The *delivery coordination process* ensures that execution of transformation is orchestrated efficiently and that redundant work is avoided. Holding the complete picture of the transformational streams of the enterprise, EA can help to reschedule, prioritize, and abort implementations; to make delivery more efficient; and to reduce disruptive impact on the organization.

Finally, the *compliance process* is the ongoing evaluation of the corporate IT platforms, relative to criteria of standards, qualities, service level agreements, and architecture requirements. Compliance assessment is performed as part of project assessments at the end of a stage/phase, but is also a general monitoring activity where the status of the EA is measured on defined principles.

Technology

The EA capability is a recursive capability. This means one of the outputs of an advanced EA capability is a coherent technological infrastructure. However, the current state of the very same infrastructure is also impacting the services EA can deliver. It is impossible to provide an accurate capability map if no one can identify what relevant capabilities exist in an area. Similarly, it is impossible to develop accurate heat maps for an IT infrastructure that holds multiple capability redundancies.

The technology element that defines the extent to which an EA capability can fulfill all purposes of the advanced EA capability is primarily the corporate digital infrastructure—the set of hardware, software, and related processes that forms the information capacity of the organization. Research shows that there are primarily three aspects of a digital infrastructure that determines how well it supports the EA: standardization, modularization, and connectivity (Duncan 1995).

Standardization means that two similar business processes should not run on two different IT systems. Having duplicate systems adds to the IT infrastructure complexity, as different systems need to be bridged to make the organization work in a coherent manner. Because the typical IT infrastructure of a firm consists of thousands of different hardware and software components, managing the interfaces between duplicate components makes it difficult to add, replace, extend, or otherwise modify components that have multiple ties to other components.

Minor deviations to a standardized IT infrastructure have limited long-term implications, but also minor deviations add cumulatively over time so that the firm has a harder and harder time managing complexity. This is why firms such as Danisco, a Danish serial acquirer in the food ingredients industry, sees their "standardization fundamentalist" attitude as critical to enabling acquisitive growth (Yetton et al. 2013). Coming from a background as a diversified conglomerate with more than 100 business units running their own IT setups, Danisco put their acquisition program on hold for several years to rebuild their IT infrastructure on a fully standardized IT platform. Once done, the time of integration dropped from several years to a few months. To enable continuous growth, Danisco safeguarded its standardized IT infrastructure as a critical growth-enabling asset.

Modularization of IT infrastructure means that the whole is broken down into parts with defined interfaces to allow for reuse of modules and modifications of components without unintended consequences multiplying across the IT infrastructure. Modularization means that an effective supply-chain system can be used to introduce best practices into an acquired organization, without necessarily having to impose sales systems and knowledge-management systems that may be inappropriate for the acquisition. Without modularization, an acquirer has to engage in duplication of IT components to achieve distinct ways of working, which adds to infrastructural complexity.

Modularization is not about trying to achieve the highest level of granularity as possible—modularization of an IT infrastructure is about finding the right level of granularity to make reutilization possible. Danske Bank, who did a series of acquisitions to execute its internationalization strategy, discovered that its initial modularization initiatives had been too ambitious. While the bank had created thousands of modules that potentially could be reused, the developers simply could not find them when needed. To manage modules, the bank decided to organize them into hierarchical structures where the main unit became something corresponding with systems capabilities that were connected to certain operational capabilities.

In the 1990s, connectivity was a real issue preventing IT integration of acquisitions. Today, because of standardization and innovation in integration technologies, it is possible to build heterogeneous IT infrastructures with hardware and software components provided by different suppliers. Connectivity is still, however, an obstacle making integration difficult. In particular, many legacy technologies were never built with the intention to coexist with other technologies in complex infrastructures. In addition, both hardware and software components still exist in different technological ecosystems. In the ecosystems, components are design to fit together and also intentionally evolve together. For example, when SAP makes updates to its software suite, the third-party community of software providers that thrive on add-on modules are informed and have to adapt the interfaces to their respective products to match the changes made by SAP. Generally, commercially available software platforms with standard implementation can be expected to have high connectivity within their technological ecosystem, while home-grown and highly customized platforms can be expected to present low levels of connectivity.

Artifacts

The value of artifacts in the context of EA is not in their existence but rather in the process of creation and usage by others. Enterprise architects are valuable in the process of enterprise transformation when they are part of a value of chain of translation from strategy to value delivery and operations. The architect's responsibility, and therefore the role of the artifacts, is to ensure that the strategic direction of executive decision-makers is expressed in a manner that is useful for those who are accountable and responsible for the delivery of this transformation and the ongoing management and operations of the enterprise capabilities.

Transformation Models

In the architect's tool kit are reference models, capability roadmaps, capability heat maps, and architecture health dashboards. Each of these artifacts are valuable when sequenced and connected correctly. For an architect, the health dashboard is an essential way to measure the current health, whether the capabilities in place are "fit for purpose," and if they are in need of adjustments and improvements.

There are two triggers that the architect can pay attention to which suggests an improvement or change is needed. The first is through continual improvement opportunities which the capability owner has detected, the other is a need for a change due to a new strategic direction based on a transformation in the enterprise. If the capabilities need adjustments or improvements, the architect can partner with the person responsible for the operations of their capability and develop a new target state architecture, which includes migration steps (projects) sequenced in such a way that they are sensitive to interdependencies and investment needs. The architect and the capability owner developing these together is critical so they jointly own the outcome of the target architecture and can learn from each other throughout the process. The architect and the capability owner can place the target state architecture migration steps on their capability roadmap to ensure it fits with other planned transformation. The architect and capability owner are also responsible for developing a business case that connects the investment made in the capability to the health dashboard, ensuring that the investment is tied directly to the improvement of the KPIs of the capability.

Lastly, the capability heath map can be used by the architect and capability owners to make investment prioritization decisions since it is likely that there are more transformation opportunities than an enterprise has the economic capacity to invest in.

Reference Models The enterprise reference model enables connectivity across a state. Figure 3.3 presents an Enterprise Reference Model for a standard gas and oil organization. In this example, the organization has laid out its capabilities across two axes, the first being the type of capability, its position within the organization, and its relation to corporate, operations, development, and acquisition functions. It also defines an axis to segregate capabilities related to its value chain, with some in the upstream part, such as the ability to extract oil from the ground, separated from the step of prospecting for new oil for extraction. Secondly, an area has been defined having to do with the manufacturing and refining processes, and lastly with marketing, sales, and trading capabilities. From this departure point, an architect can now determine which of these capabilities is going to be impacted by the transformation and double-click on them to understand what business processes, systems, and technology capabilities will need to be transformed. With many organizations that undergo multiple transformation at the same time, the architects can also determine any interdependencies across these capabilities and take into account any issues and risks, making the likelihood of success that much greater. Once the target state has been defined, the architects can build a case with business leaders and execution teams that connects the intended or desired target state with the planning/definition part of program development.

To allow architects the opportunity to document the target state of the enterprise, it is important for them to maintain an up-to-date reference model that shows the current state of the enterprise and where transformation is already under way. In other words, it connects the EA together. In traditional EA groups, this reference model is updated on a recurring basis both in areas of transformation and where no transformation is occurring, leading to wasted architecture resources and stale documents that are never used. Rather, EA should focus on updating the reference model in only those areas where transformation is occurring and make progressive updates over time. A reference model is an abstract framework or domain-specific ontology consisting of an interlinked set of clearly defined concepts produced to encourage clear communication.

A reference model can represent the component parts of any consistent idea from business functions to system components, as long as it represents a complete set. This frame of reference can then be used to communicate ideas clearly among members of the same community. They are often illustrated as a set of concepts with some indication of the relationships between concepts.

Capability Roadmaps Complementing the reference model, the capability roadmap (Fig. 3.4) enables connectivity across time, ensuring that capabilities are sequenced and paced correctly and any interdependencies are identified. Capability roadmaps

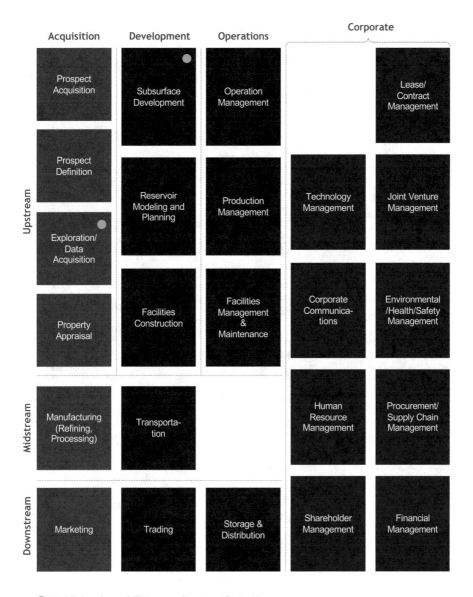

Fig. 3.3 An example of capabilities in an oil and gas company

show the development plans for capabilities and allow architects to focus their attention on specific capabilities that need attention in an organizational transformation. Capability roadmaps also enable decision-makers to determine the relative difficulty of a transformation and the options to consider along with a cost estimate. The roadmaps take into account other ongoing transformations in each capability

Strategy & Supporting Capabilities			Channel Partner Platforms-Foundation	Channel Partner Platforms-NextGen	
FY17	Q4		POC Report migration Strategy		
			PMC- data Analysis	Program migration Strategy	
FY18	Q1			Pega planning	
	Q2		• Pilot- reporting for Certs, • Rebates & Service Performance Metrics (up to 10 reports) • Limited Availability to select few partners • Reports based on Legacy data model		• Pega foundation release • Rules framework
	Q3	PMART Reporting	• General availability to all partners • General reporting • Additional reports for Pilot • Limited availability to select few partners • Reports based on legacy data model	• Program admin & rebate processing (core capabilities) • Program planning (sandbox)	• Cert/Spec/ ATP/CMSP partner enrollment capabilities • Integrated workflow
	Q3	Service Performance Metrics	• General availability to all partners • Reporting optimization due to cert/spec & rebate data model changes • Cert/ spec & rebates reporting • Limited availability to selected few partners • Reports based on Next Gen data model	• Program admin and rebate processing (additional capabilities) • Start onboarding of programs	All internal capabilities supporting the Cert/Spec/ATP/ CMSP requirements
FY19	Q1	• Reporting optimization • Analytics capabilities			Channel partner onboarding

Fig. 3.4 An example of a capability roadmap

view. The integration activities are therefore not separate and unique transformation activities but are built into the general capability roadmaps for each part of the EA.

Capability Heat Maps Understanding the overall health of each business and technical capability that makes up the enterprise enables the architect to align the investment proposals and changes proposed in the roadmaps to ensure that the correct capabilities are invested in. The capability heat map (Fig. 3.5) is a graphical representation of the entire enterprise that allows decision-makers to get a complete picture not only of the health of each capability but also its strategic importance in delivering value to customers and shareholders. The heat map ensures that the decision-makers are aware of the risk, value, readiness, and architectural fit to the enterprise.

Capability Health Dashboards An architecture health dashboard is a tool to assess the ongoing health of the EA. In the generic representation of what such a health dashboard can look like (Fig. 3.6), it presents 14 strategic portfolios which are important to the enterprise. Each is measured in terms of architecture health in the following four areas: risk, policy, maturity, and interdependence. Each strategic portfolio includes the integration activities required to complete the ongoing transformation activities in the organization. This enables the executive leadership team to see the full scope of transformation within the enterprise rather than a siloed view of the integration activities separate from other transformational activities. With this tool the executives can determine how the components involved in transformations are being dealt with beyond the integration life cycle, and success can be measured based on these metrics.

Solution Models

Connecting the overarching strategic intent and target state to the delivery team who will carry out the development of new capabilities or the modification of existing ones will need more than the high-level roadmaps to ensure the execution of the solution is in line with the overall target architecture. Solution models are developed at the level of business process, data flow, or systems interaction to document the detailed level of the change.

Requirement Models These models detail the demands on business and technology capabilities. Detailed requirements can be organized into a hierarchy culminating in a high-level requirement, so that satisfying each of the detailed requirements results in meeting the higher-level requirements and ultimately the top-level requirement. This hierarchical structure helps manage the complexity of large systems with thousands of requirements and many processes being developed to implement the requirements.

Use Case Models These models drill to swim-lane models for each use case/process. The models tend to focus on system flows more than Business Workflows at this level, as the models are for developers to build out system processing.

Management Control Reporting	Core Business	Generic Support Functions	Internal Control Functions
Planning	Distribution	Input Management	HR Management
Reporting	Proposition	Business Partner Management	Facility Management
Risk Management	Distribution Channels	Financial Management	Financial Management
Heatmap Key / High Priority	Production	Reinsurance	Employee Event management
Moderate Priority / Low Priority	Primary Purchasing	Incentives & Commissions	Secondary Purchasing
Architectural Fit		Document Management	IT Management
Value		Output Management	Communications Management
Risk		Financial Processing	

Heatmap Key

- High Priority
- Moderate Priority
- Low Priority

Architectural Fit

- (A) Very High
- (A) High
- A Moderate
- (A) Low
- (A) Very Low

Value

- (V) Very High
- (V) High
- V Moderate
- (V) Low
- (V) Very Low

Risk

- (R) Very High
- (R) Low
- R Moderate
- (R) High
- (R) Very High

Readiness

- (Re) Very High
- (Re) High
- Re Moderate
- (Re) Low
- (Re) Very Low

Fig. 3.5 An example of a capability heat map

Business Interaction Models Shows how users and systems interact within a high-level business ecosystem and drill to Deployment Models for each System and show the Code Modules, Services, and Interfaces for a single high-level system.

Deployment Models These are Component Diagrams that show the Code Modules, Services, and Interfaces and their interaction dependencies. These are not production

Architecture Health Dashboard

On track ●
At risk ▲
Risk w/o mitigation ▪

Health Report:	Policy	Dependencies	Arch Maturity	Risks	Invest-ment
Strategies					
Next Generation Network	▲	▲	●	▲	▲
Infrastructure & Platform Service Delivery	▲	▲	▲	▲	▲
Global Data Center	▲	▲	●	▲	▲

Architecture Maturity	SIE Models			Business & IT Arch Alignment (Connecting CNI- O S T)	
S view Adoption	Expected total number of SIEs	Target SIEs-WIP	Target SIEs-Published	% of Systems mapped to Operational Capabilities	% of System Mapped to Technology Platform
FY-14	-NA-	-NA-	-NA-	-NA-	-NA-
FY-15	5	1	0	0	0

T-view Adoption	Actual # of current Technology Platforms	Expected # of new technology platform	% Tech platforms with TRM & Lifecycles	Expected # of new network models	New Network Models-WIP	New Network Models-Published
FY-14	44	63	78%	46	1	45
FY-15	119	12	73%	14	1	0

Fig. 3.6 An example of a health dashboard

deployment models, as they do not assume IP addressing, server names, etc. They are an architectural model of how the system works.

Work Breakdown Models These models are deliverable-oriented decomposition of a project into smaller components. A work breakdown model organizes a major transformation in manageable sections. The output of an element in the model may be a product, data, system, service, or any combination thereof.

Having established the challenges of acquisitive growth and defined the workings of an advanced EA capability, the following sections address how such a capability can be leveraged throughout the acquisition process. To do so requires full activation of the holistic and engaged capability qualities.

Chapter Key Points

- EA is uniquely positioned to organize, structure, and lead transformational efforts in a digital world.
- EA has a very different purpose in different organizations.
- An advanced EA capability has broken free from the technical heritage, to become a driver of technical and organizational change.
- The holistic quality refers to the span of architecting practice from fundamental technology layers to business strategy layers.
- The engaged quality refers to the direct and intentional engagement in transformations.
- EA people, processes, and technology form EA capacities that enable EA qualities.
- EA artifacts are the transformation and solutions model that architects produce when architecting.

References

Bhogill, P., & Covington, B. (2011). The importance of enterprise architecture to mergers and acquisitions. *Oracle Experiences in Enterprise Architecture*. Accessed October 28, 2019, from www.oracle.com/us/products/consulting/enterprise-architecture-services/oeea-mergers-305843.html

Duncan, N. B. (1995). Capturing flexibility of information technology infrastructure: A study of resource characteristics and their measure. *Journal of Management Information Systems, 12*(2), 37–57.

LSA Global. (2019). *Do not overthink business strategy as a leader*. Accessed October 28, 2019, from https://lsaglobal.com/blog/not-overthink-business-strategy/

Ross, J. W., Weill, P., & Robertson, D. (2006). *Enterprise architecture as strategy: Creating a foundation for business execution*. Boston, MA: Harvard Business Press.

Yetton, P., Henningsson, S., & Bjorn-Andersen, N. (2013). Ready to acquire': IT resources for a growth-by-acquisition strategy. *MIS Quarterly Executive, 12*(1), 19–35.

Part II
Enterprise Architecture in the Acquisition Process

Having set the foundations by presenting the acquisition challenge and the workings of an advanced EA capability, we now turn to how EA can be leveraged in the different phases of an acquisition process. Whether it is in the preparation, setting the foundation for growth, in the actual enactment of the acquisition, or in the aftermath care of the residual effects, EA can make a real impact. Here, we detail the touchpoints between the acquisition process and EA, and the activities that realize EA's possible impact.

Chapter 4
Preparation: *Positioning* the Organization

When lightning strikes and an acquisition is announced, many firms are severely unprepared for what is to come. Because of the sensitivity of acquisitions, deal negotiation is typically only the concern of a small, dedicated group of people. Rumors of a possible acquisition can increase the market valuation of the target—and impact the share price of the acquirer negatively. Many managers in an acquiring firm will hear about an acquisition only weeks before a deal is settled, or even read about it in the press after it has happened. Therefore, managers are typically unprepared for what is to come.

When the deal is settled it is in many ways too late to act. A substantive part of the acquisition outcome is defined already by the preconditions at the time of signing a deal: the acquirer's ability to accommodate the new business practices and technical infrastructure that the target might bring, its awareness of the existing business processes that can be reimplemented in the target, the internal collaboration structure and organizational culture permitting exploitation of new opportunities, etc. The improvement of these and other critical conditions is measured in years, not weeks. Therefore, to avoid time-consuming improvements in the period leading up to an acquisition, a prospective acquirer should preemptively focus on positioning the organization to be ready to acquire.

Acquisitions come in many forms and flavors, ranging from mega mergers of rivals to directed efforts targeted at specific technologies. Being ready to acquire does not mean that the acquirer should be ready for anything at any time. This would be too expensive, and probably not even feasible. Being ready to acquire means that the organization is ready to embrace a defined set of growth options in certain areas. It means that the conditions to embrace these specific options are appropriately managed. It means that the resources to act are identified and secured, so when lightning strikes the acquirer is ready to hit the ground running.

Being able to position the firm for relevant acquisitions is about the avoidance of problems, rather than being better at solving the problems that arise during an acquisition. The ability to proactively position the firm to deal with the challenges

© Springer Nature Switzerland AG 2020

S. Henningsson, G. N. Toppenberg, *Architecting Growth in the Digital Era*,
https://doi.org/10.1007/978-3-030-39482-0_4

that will come is something that sets experienced acquirers apart from many novice acquirers. To illustrate this, let us take a look at the serial acquirer Cisco Systems.

At Cisco Systems, acquisitions form an integrated component of the corporate strategy. This multinational corporation was founded by two computer scientists from Stanford University in 1984, as a business primarily centered in networking equipment and related services. By 2016, Cisco had grown to 72,000 employees with revenues of $49 billion. and moved its headquarters to Silicon Valley in San Jose, California. Much of this growth, going from a small router manufacturer to a global network business, was achieved through acquisitions. Seven years after its inception, Cisco made its first acquisition. During the following 2 years another 10 firms were added to the organization. By 2016, the company had completed more than 185 acquisitions,[1] continuing to acquire at a pace of 5–10 acquisitions per year.

Cisco developed an advanced acquisition capability that gave it the reputation of an acquirer that repeatedly identified and captured value through its acquisition process. However, at times Cisco struggled with its acquisition program. In particular, during the mid-1990s and 2000s, the organizational preconditions did not permit efficient integration of the acquisitions that were made. To enable acquisition-based growth, in both the mid-1990s and 2000s (Austin et al. 2002), Cisco undertook major organizational restructuring to make the company "acquisition ready." In order to understand how they accomplished this, let us take a look at some of the different types of acquisitions the company performed.

Among the many acquisitions by Cisco, there are three specific types that have been particularly prevalent. First, acquisitions to extend into a new market adjacency (solution extension). Second, acquisitions to acquire "tech and talent" which is a strategy to acquire specific engineering groups or adding a piece of digital technology, such as a *bolt-on*, to existing technology that Cisco sells. Third, Cisco started to acquire companies that were emerging, and investing in a technology that could disrupt its own solutions to existing customers. Cisco made these acquisitions to stay ahead of the technology trends – to disrupt themselves before someone else did.

Already in 2006, Cisco started to build the preconditions to enable these kinds of acquisitions. As part of this journey, Cisco decided to reconsider its EA capability and to use it as a vehicle to position the company to be ready to acquire (Kalbag and Narasimhan 2012). EA at Cisco was, until the late 2000s, focused on the activities surrounding technology operation. EA provided a way for IT architects and leaders to align technology enablement to the continuously complex business models that were being maintained. However, given the accelerated pace of change in the technology industry and the growing number of acquisitions Cisco made, it was unable to sustain this pace without a more elaborated approach to the alignment of business and technical architectures. Consequently, in 2009 Cisco started to explore the possibilities and benefits of a corporate EA capability that included both business and technical architecture and aimed to help planning for business transformation at the enterprise scale (see Box 4.1) (Cisco 2014). The EA capability at Cisco became a

---

[1]http://en.wikipedia.org/wiki/List_of_acquisitions_by_Cisco_Systems

key component of the translation of business vision and strategy into effective enterprise change by creating, communicating, and improving the key requirements, principles, and models that described the enterprise's future state and enabled its evolution.

Box 4.1 Cisco's EA Capability, as of 2016 Cisco's EA capability built on the BOST *architectural framework*, which included Business, Operations, System, and Technology views, supported by a *reference architecture* and a well-defined *methodology*. The four views of the BOST framework represented different layers within an enterprise, and there were five different types of models within each view:

- The Business view is focused on the market, and included the product, market, and resource models. This was where Cisco identified what products were part of its portfolio, what markets it served, and the resources needed to accomplish its mission.
- The Operations view included models that described operations processes such as supply chain, financial reporting, human resources, and organizational models.
- The Systems view included the application relationship models and the information exchange diagrams that showed how data is transacted between systems.
- The Technology view included the technological infrastructure models, including device and network models.

At Cisco, EA had an orchestrating role that was enabled by structurally positioning EA as a cross-functional capability, sitting between the business and IT functions. In 2016, 70 people were working in various roles related to systems and technology architecture, and 30 people were employed to manage business and operations architecture. The head of business architecture reported to the COO and was responsible for the business and operations view of the architecture. The head of technology architecture reported to the CIO and was responsible for the systems and technology views.

The business and technology side of the EA capability was coupled through the link between basic service functions architects and chief architects who typically worked in pairs with one stack of capabilities ranging from business to technological enablement. For example, one pair of architects at this level had responsibility for Cisco's software consumptions models, which specified the four ways by which Cisco offered software to its customers. Managing changes related to these capabilities, and to the enabling stack of operational, systems, and technology capabilities was the responsibility of the EA pair.

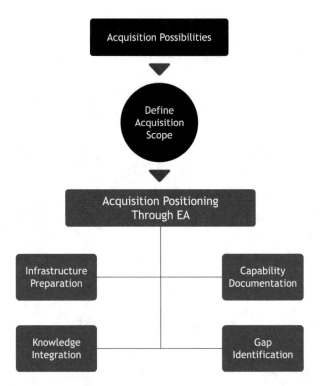

Fig. 4.1 Acquisition positioning through EA

Pre-acquisition preparation at Cisco was an ongoing activity and not specific to any particular acquisition. The ongoing pre-acquisition preparation enabled the firm to hit the ground running in any business transformation, avoiding the need to first prepare critical resources or to document the as-is scenario. The benefits of the preparatory work were related to speed, rather than cost. For Cisco, because of the types of acquisitions made, speed in the acquisition process (expressed in the evaluation criteria of time to orderability and time to completion) was of utmost importance.

Figure 4.1 presents a schematic process for how EA is engaged in positioning a company to be ready to acquire. The process starts with defining the set of acquisitions that the company may want to achieve, to guide the building of growth options. Depending on how the acquisition scope is defined, the positioning should focus on slightly different enabling conditions. In Cisco and other acquirers, the EA capability can contribute to positioning the firm to be ready to acquire through five different activities: *infrastructure preparation*, *documentation*, *knowledge integration*, *gap exposure*, and *platformization* (Table 4.1). The last one would be particularly applicable for acquisitions aimed at divested business units, because it is a mechanism that enables rapid accommodation of such acquisitions. Engaging EA in these

Table 4.1 EA in the preparation for future acquisitions

EA activity	Purpose	Critical accomplishments
Infrastructure preparation	Getting the IT infrastructure ready for acquisitions	Ongoing control activities to ensure that no transformational or development activities compromise the IT infrastructure flexibility
Documentation	Documenting the as-is situation	Ongoing documentation of the organization, including, appropriate resource and organizational models
Knowledge integration	Establish working connection across organizational layers	Working closely in joint teams with business and technology partners, the EA function promotes an ongoing awareness of the possibilities and constraints of the other partner
Gap exposure	Highlight gaps in the capability landscape	Feed into the acquisition unit capabilities that could be attractive acquisition targets to complement the existing portfolio
Platformization	Separate common core application from business-unit-specific applications	Determine what is each business unit's unique value proposition and what is the common corporate strategy

activities should be done with respect to the specific set of acquisitions the company can envision in the future, to build options for growth. Let us take a look at these activities in more depth.

Infrastructure Preparation

In the 1990s, when firms started to be more and more dependent on their IT systems, research on the topic of IT integration in acquisition grew. At this time, the problems of IT integration emerged as a neglected and important explanation to the hardships of substantiating acquisition benefits. Incompatible systems and network technologies caused delays and additional costs. Because many large organizations were highly diversified they were run as sets of independent businesses with their own enabling set of IT systems. Incompatible technological systems made it impossible to reap operational synergies across business units.

Following a series of studies that focused on the emergence of IT-related barriers to efficient acquisitions, the general conclusion was made that IT fit should be considered to an equal extent as any other resource fit in the consideration of an acquisition. The proactive acquirer should only acquire targets that are technically compatible with the acquirer, to enable smooth IT integration. The acquisition of a technically incompatible target would require a fundamental rebuild on the IT platform acquisition, which would mean all of the uncertainties and expenses such a project would bring.

Today, the argument to assess IT fit is still made and if brought into the early stage of the acquisition process, some IT organizations would still be focusing on the technical details of the hardship of managing diverse technologies in heterogeneous IT infrastructure. For many business managers and, luckily, for many IT managers, the solution that IT dictates to what growth options a firm should pursue seems absurd. The tail does not wag the dog and IT should enable rather than constrain business strategies. In the acquisition context, this is done by building the IT infrastructures that are flexible in the right ways to meet the organization's ambitions to grow. The three general features that make an IT infrastructure flexible (*standardization*, *modularization*, and *connectivity*) are described in Chap. 3.

An advanced EA capability can and should contribute to preparing a scalable IT infrastructure. Let us go back to our example, Cisco. Cisco's first major platform project in the late 1990s is described in detail in a Harvard Business Case (Austin et al. 2002) as necessary to sustain continued growth. This project put in place an effective but monolithic IT platform that allowed a growth program for a network manufacturer. As the firm reoriented itself, away from the manufacturing logic, to innovation-based competition of a high-tech company, a second platform project was required in 2005. The justification was that the previously lean platform had become "*cost-prohibitive for supporting Cisco's growth and evolving business requirements*" (Cisco 2007).

In the work with the new platform, EA contributed to the standardization, modularization, and connectivity of the infrastructure. Drawing on the BOST framework (see Box 4.1), EA mapped the business and technology capabilities across the company. For each capability, EA was tasked and mandated to ensure standardization—there should only exist a limited set of business capabilities, and they should only be supported by a standardized set of operational, systems, and technology capabilities. EA did not decide which business capabilities to standardize on, but highlighted redundancies and showed potential for standardization.

To ensure connectivity of the IT infrastructure, the EA team constantly monitored the technological components that were introduced. When IT components were introduced into the systems or technology level of the EA framework, these components were assessed for how well they could be integrated with Cisco's other IT resources, their level of conformity with Cisco standards, and possible integration scenarios. Ensuring the infrastructural integrity allowed for relatively effortless extension and expansion of the existing IT infrastructure when Cisco made an acquisition.

The benefits of this revitalized EA function for infrastructure preparation can be illustrated with Cisco's work with software consumption models. In 2007, Cisco offered software to their customers in 32 different ways. Starting in 2007, Cisco standardized on four consumption models: own up front, leasing, software as a service, and utility. It was the work of the EA function that highlighted the 32 consumption models and suggested that these actually corresponded to only four unique business capabilities.

EA could also show that these four business capabilities could be supported by standardized operational systems and technology capabilities at a much lower cost.

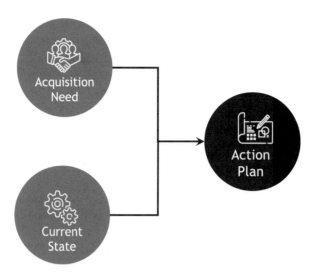

Fig. 4.2 Creating an action plan for infrastructure preparation

By defining specific service owners and allocating costs directly to the services, incitements were created for making the transition to shared capabilities. In addition, a specific pair of business and technology architects was given the task and authority to ensure that the four software consumption models remained the only models, regardless of which organizational transformations occurred. For acquisitions, this meant that all future acquisitions would fit into the architecture.

How Cisco ensured infrastructure preparation through EA was not related to any specific acquisition. Instead, it was a deliberate action of considering the current state in light of anticipated needs. The logical outcome of this was an action plan, devising some actions that needed to be carried out right away and others that could wait until an specific type of acquisition actually happened. In some areas it was not needed to actually invest in scalability until it was a fact that scale was indeed needed (Fig. 4.2). Recall, the infrastructure was built to be able to act when an acquisition target was identified and a deal was secured. For example, when Cisco evaluated a potential acquisition in 2012, it offered four standardized consumption models, which were easy to redeploy in different contexts. Cisco could then draw on the scalable infrastructure to quickly assess how the consumption models matched the way the target was doing business, and then eventually redeploy the technology capabilities to support the target with preexisting systems and technology capabilities.

Back when the company had 32 different consumption models, which were all supported by distinct sets of operational, systems, and technology capabilities, no one even knew where these 32 consumption models were, or how they were enabled. In consequence, even if there had been a matching consumption model and suitable enabling capabilities within Cisco, no one would have known. In this case, acquiring a new company would have led to the addition of a 33rd consumption model and new enabling software and hardware, making the infrastructure even more rigid. Using the advanced EA capability to standardize and oversee the right level of modularization of enabling capabilities, Cisco efficiently reused the existing infrastructure without compromising the long-term agility of the company.

Documentation

When an acquisition deal is assessed, the potential acquirer typically has only a few weeks to conclude the assessment and present an offer. During these weeks the team working with the bid needs to identify all possible sources for synergy creation between the target as well as all the potential roadblocks to realizing these synergies. For the task of understanding the target, time is already very short. At the same time, trying to model its own enterprise is impossible. So, if no documentation of the current state of the acquirer exists, estimates about synergies and roadblocks will be merely guesses.

At Cisco, the acquisitions were facilitated by the EA team maintaining up-to-date documentation of available resources and their dependencies in the reference models. Creating this documentation when an acquisition target is already identified could severely delay the process of assessing the match between the two organizations or could significantly compromise the matching because of incorrect capability models. Because of the existing documentation at Cisco at the start of an acquisition, the transformation team was able to avoid having to first document the as-is scenario.

Using the relevant Cisco capability models as a starting point, the acquisition team investigated the practice of the acquisition according to the Cisco template for due diligence. Capability heat maps (see Chap. 3) identifying the areas that needed particular attention were developed. These indicated areas in Cisco's capability models, where deviations in target's behavior could have significant implications for time to orderability, time to completion, and cost savings. In many areas, for example, marketing, supply chain management, or financial control, deviations would not be important. Differences would not threaten value creation. In contrast, the software consumption model was one area where differences could be critical.

For instance, a difference once was identified by the acquisition team in how the target provided their software to customers, compared to the existing practice in Cisco in a business area. Whereas Cisco used partners to sell their services, the target had direct relations with clients. EA was engaged to see if this could constitute a roadblock to integration and, if necessary, to develop a capability model for the target in this particular area.

A pair of business and technology architects responsible for Cisco's capability models was tasked with the work. Sufficient information was obtained to sketch out the workings of the target's consumption model and to verify that it would be possible to support it with preexisting operational systems and technical capabilities. Because EA could rapidly assure the acquisition team that Cisco already provided the capabilities to support the target's software consumption model software, the issue was removed from the list of acquisition risks.

Furthermore, the intended acquisition's unique consumption model was identified as an opportunity for reverse integration. Cisco's corresponding business could learn how to reach customers without partners. It was, however, decided to keep the business view independent initially and mobilize Cisco's pre-acquisition capabilities in the operating, systems, and technology views to enable the dual-mode business approach.

Knowledge Integration

Acquisitions are cross-layer activities, operating in parallel dimensions. The reasons for the deal are generated at the business level, but the causes as to why a deal does not live up to expectations commonly originates at the technical layers of the organizations.

However, a closer examination of the causes of why the technical integration becomes problematic commonly points back to the business layers. Poorly communicated acquisition objectives, paradoxical organizational integration objectives, insufficient acquisition planning, changing requirements and overall poor leadership in the acquisition project are among the most cited factors for unsuccessful IT integration. Only to a very minor extent do problems originate in technological issues such as developer incompetence or incompatible technologies.

So, what then are the conditions that contribute positively to technological integration success? One such condition is the leveraging of preexisting cross-functional teams. At Cisco the EA function was organized in teams working on the four levels in the EA framework together. The teams consisted of one partner focusing primarily on the Business and Operations levels of the EA framework reporting to the Chief Operating Officer (COO), and one partner with primary responsibility for the Systems and Technology levels reporting to the Chief Information Officer (CIO). The close partnerships ensured that there was ongoing knowledge integration between the technology and business areas of the organization. Each partner was constantly getting a better understanding of the implications that the decisions taken had for the other partner, and the possibility that the partner had to respond to demands put on them. In an acquisition, understanding how the business and operational capabilities interact and what information flows between them helped the EA team to identify areas of opportunity and concern prior to the integration and helped Cisco to later plan extra efforts in those areas of concern in addition to leveraging the areas of opportunity. As we can see, through promoting interaction between business and technology functions, EA enabled a better understanding of the existing opportunities and constraints.

Gap Exposure

An additional use of the EA function in the pre-acquisition preparation phase is the highlighting of areas where the acquirer is missing capabilities. Identifying capability gaps consists of a trigger for target search. Capability gaps can be of two kinds. On one hand, it can be a business capability that is clearly missing from the portfolio that makes customers prefer other providers. But a capability gap can also be a new business capability for which the enablement already exists, and for which there are then likely substantial cost synergies to realize in an acquisition.

At Cisco, this proactive use of EA fed into the acquisition division, which was responsible for scanning the environment for acquisition targets. If targets emerged that fitted the identified gaps, the acquisition division started to investigate the prospect of filling the capability gap through acquisition. For instance, in one acquisition, the capability model assisted in demonstrating the need to build or acquire additional capabilities in the video area, and what capabilities would complement the existing capabilities. Consequently, when a company emerged as a possible acquisition target, the recognized need to reinforce the area was a contributing reason to look further into the prospects of the deal.

Platformization

Finally, EA can be engaged in the process of preparation by guiding the platformization of an IT landscape. A typical IT landscape is the product of many years of incremental additions, including legacy systems that were never built to accommodate change. A platformization activity decouples the landscape into two layers, one core layer and one peripheral layer. This allows a corporation to run multiple business units on a common platform that allows the corporate to compete as a whole, and not only as a set of independent businesses. The corporate core layer will include the applications shared across the corporation, while the peripheral layer contains the business-unit-specific applications. If the corporation is to provide one single face to its customer, then a customer management system is put in the corporate core layer to enable this. If each business unit has a different approach to customer interactions and acts in distinct markets, then the customer management systems are kept at the business unit level (Fig. 4.3).

Platformization an IT landscape is critical to accommodate new business units. There are two scenarios where this is useful. The first is when a multibusiness organization acquirers as stand-alone business for scope. Here, the IT enablement of acquired business would be partitioned into components matching the corporate core and the business unit peripheral layer. Thus with the unique IT enablement of a business unit and with support of corporate IT enablement the acquired business could be established as a new business unit.

The second scenario where platformization plays a key role is in acquisitions of divestments, where the acquired unit would be sold off without the IT enablement provided by the parent. Platformization makes it possible to accommodate this

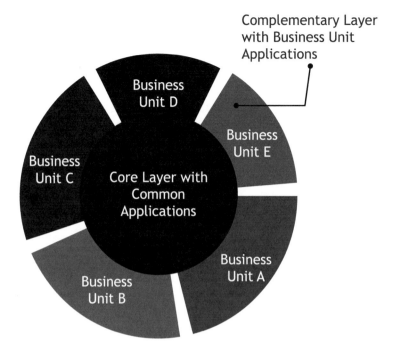

Fig. 4.3 Platformization of the IT infrastructure

business unit with its own unique business unit applications. An integration project that first needed to disentangle the corporate and business-unit-specific applications would be costly and time consuming. Likely, such a project would drag out longer than the availability of transition service agreement with the vendor last. Under these conditions, a divestment acquisition that increases business scope would in practice be impossible to implement.

At Cisco, the decoupling of applications that made Cisco act as single corporation towards customers from the business-unit-specific applications was part of the transformational work by EA starting in 2006. Having established an understanding of what was corporate and what was business unit specific allowed EA to execute the decoupling in practice. Here EA played an instrumental role in guiding the work by documenting the current state and visualizing the to-be state. Ultimately, what went into each layer was a business and not architectural decision, but EA ensured that systems and technology enablement was adjusted to business developments.

Chapter Key Points

- The pre-acquisition preparation is an ongoing activity and not specific to any particular acquisition.
- The benefits of including EA in the preparation is related to speed rather than cost.

- In the preparation phase of the acquisition, EA can contribute to:
  - *Infrastructure preparation* by ensuring that the IT infrastructure becomes ready to build further on
  - *Documentation* of the as-is situation by developing capability maps and reference models
  - *Knowledge integration* by establishing working connections across the organizational layers of a company
  - *Gap exposure* through highlighting gaps in the organizational capability landscape that can be addressed through acquisitions
  - *Platformization* to allow for carve-out business units and multibusiness organization

References

Austin, R. D., Nolan, R. L., & Cotteleer M. J. (2002). Cisco Systems, Inc.: Implementing ERP. *Harvard Business School Cases* (699022).

Cisco. (2007). Business applications case study: How Cisco IT upgraded its ERP manufacturing and finance modules. *Cisco Case Studies.*

Cisco. (2014). Enterprise architecture. *Cisco IT Insights.* Accessed October 28, 2019, from https://www.cisco.com/c/dam/en_us/about/ciscoitatwork/business_of_it/docs/i-boit-05192014-enterprise-architecture.pdf

Kalbag, A., & Narasimhan, S. (2012). Enterprise architecture and IT service management. *Business Transformation Through Architectures.* Accessed October 28, 2019, from https://www.cisco.com/c/en/us/solutions/collateral/enterprise/cisco-on-cisco/Cisco_IT_Trends_in_IT_Article_Ent_Architecture_IT_Service_Management.html

Chapter 5
Target Selection: *Identifying* Value

Acquisitions are all about creating synergistic effects between two organizational entities. To get ownership of another business, the acquirer typically needs to pay a premium compared to what the target is valued in the market. The market price of a company is based on the minimum price that any of the shareholders are ready to accept for a share. The acquisition price is in contrast based on the minimum price that some 90–95% of the shareholders will accept. This is naturally much higher than the lowest share price. Therefore, acquisition prices that are much over the market price are common.

The challenge of selecting a target is finding an organization where the combined firms have the potential to create more value together than as separate entities. Target selection is about understanding, both at a high strategic level and at a more granular operational level, the effect of bundling the two: the potential synergies, transformation needs, and any barrier that can impede the creation of synergies (Fig. 5.1). Getting this wrong is extremely expensive as a futile integration project will drain resources, employee morale, and managerial attention from the involved parties for several years and then, at its best, only have moved both the organizations sideways. In the worst-case scenario, valuable skills, teams, processes, and cultures have been destroyed in the process.

Target selection is notoriously difficult for several reasons. One is the lack of information for forming adequate decisions. Competition laws and strategic confidentially limits what can be shared between the parties before the deal has been reached and is approved by legal authorities. In many instances, the companies involved in acquisitions may have some sort of competitive relation before the transaction, which makes them further reluctant to expose themselves in case the deal is aborted.

The time pressure that commonly exists to form decisions further complicates the challenge of having sparse information. In a typical acquisition process, the due diligence preceding a bid takes place over a few, very intensive weeks where the prospective acquirer frantically scrambles together clues about how the target can complement its current operation and the issues that could materialize in the

© Springer Nature Switzerland AG 2020
S. Henningsson, G. N. Toppenberg, *Architecting Growth in the Digital Era*,
https://doi.org/10.1007/978-3-030-39482-0_5

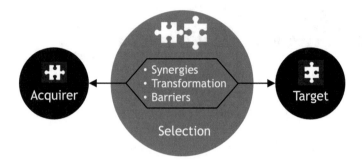

Fig. 5.1   Estimating the value potential in target selection

realization of this value. Several different bidders may be involved, adding to the selection phase the challenge of finding the threshold price for the acquisition to make sense.

An advanced EA capability can effectively ease the challenge of estimating the actual value of the target for a specific acquirer. Essentially, this capacity of EA rests on the ability to forecast complementary aspects between two organizations at the capability level. Given the time pressure, the investigation of capability complementarity can never be complete or exhaustive. The objective is not to have the senior management team sit down with detailed capability maps of both companies where the value is calculated capability by capability. What can be achieved through the use of EA is a high-level understanding of where the critical areas are, where value can be created or destroyed, and then conduct detailed investigation of those specific areas.

To do this, EA can engage in seven distinct activities within the selection phase: *business case estimation, transformation needs assessment, roadblock analysis, discovery of reverse integration potential, suite analysis, platform consistency modelling*, and *identification of nontransferable enablers* (Table 5.1). The first five activities collectively contribute towards understanding the complementarities, and is fundamental for estimating synergistic effects and identifying the barriers that must be overcome to substantiate acquisition benefits. These five activities would be relevant to all acquisitions with an integration need. The last two activities would be unique to the acquisition of a divestment, where some IT resource can be expected not be part of the deal. In this situation it is critical to assess pre-acquisitions if what is not transferred could barrier any synergy or the operational capacity of the acquisition. Let us take a closer look at these seven activities.

Business Case Estimation

Unreliable estimations of value and effort is a chronic disease in many organizations. Beyond the impacts on cost and schedule, unreliable estimates can also lead to a failure to deliver, and leave a lasting negative perception and lack of confidence

Table 5.1 EA in the selection of acquisition targets

EA activity	Purpose	Critical accomplishments
Business case estimation	Valuation of combinatory potential	EA artifacts help to determine the business and operational capabilities in place that would support the new business models being acquired. They are also used to determine which elements of the acquisition would be integrated wholly and which would remain stand-alone.
Transformation needs assessment	Cost estimation for the transformation needed to leverage potential synergistic effects	By understanding the transformation needed to integrate the desired elements the EA team is able to define programs with estimates across all four views needed to complete the integration and account for conflicting developments in the affected capabilities.
Roadblock analysis	Revelation of roadblocks that could hinder synergy realization	Acquisitions have potential roadblocks for realization in the preservation of what makes the target unique. The EA team can verify if it is possible to retain separate business capabilities, while still redeploying existing operational, systems, and technical capabilities.
Discovery of reverse integration potential	Exposure of the possibilities to redeploy capabilities from the acquisition	The preservation and redeployment of seemingly superior business capabilities in the target, compared to the acquirer's preexisting capabilities is attractive. EA can assess if the redeployment is possible given extant supporting capabilities in the acquirer.
Suite analysis	Product/service/solution offering overlap and analysis	EA can assist in the investigation of whether the target's digital offerings contribute to the suite of integrated offerings in the acquirer by evaluating the potential product integration issues and opportunities from the point of view of a customer.
Platform consistency modelling	Determine if the platform support of a divestment acquisition matches acquirer platform	Through capability models of corporation and business units, EA can assist in identifying between the platform enablement that a divested unit received from its current parent company and what the acquirer can offer.
Identification of nontransferable enablers	To avoid losing critically enabling IT resources in the acquisition of divestments	Identification of IT assets that are nontransferable from the acquirer because of technical complexity, legal reasons, or licenses and for which transition service agreements needs to be negotiated.

among leadership, customers, and stakeholders. In acquisitions, tales from the trenches tell us about business case estimates that start to live their own lives after being made public and the acquisition has been announced. For example, when two US oil and gas companies merged, the companies announced to Wall Street that it would create cost savings in the range of US$300 million annually within 18 months. The market analysts then kept their eyes on those figures, asking at each quarterly report about the progress and how much had been saved thus far. Any significant deviation led to an immediate push back on the valuation of the company. The delay and lack of cost synergy realization was not only seen as a sign that this particular deal wouldn't turn out as good as anticipated, but more importantly as a sign that the company was not a very skillful acquirer. With the ongoing consolidation in the industry, this company was deemed poorly positioned to continue its growth and punished for this in its valuation.

With pressures from shareholders and the board, managers tend to get fixated on accomplishing the business case estimates even if that requires cutting off an arm and a leg. A sales capability that shows signs of being a unique asset to the target company, offering a distinct go-to-market strategy that suits its extant customer base, gets absorbed into a larger, generic sales organization. A local innovation capability that is effective within a particular market segment is moved into a general R&D function. These consolidations save money in the short run. Signs that this may not be good in the long term can be visible, but given the commitment to the initial estimate and the punishment for deviation, the economically justifiable decision is still to push forward. Where things went wrong in the first place was in the business case estimation.

What EA can provide in relation to business case estimation is the creation of the starting points for the estimation and an articulation of the post-acquisition to-be scenario. Two starting points are needed. The first is the as-is description of the acquirer. This would typically be the global reference model at a high level, showing how the acquirer itself competes. This model is unlikely to be complete and up to date in all areas, but if EA has been involved in the preparation activities, the reference model could be of reasonable quality in the areas where acquisitive growth is expected. For example, when the Danish conglomerate Danisco decided to abandon its highly diversified operation to focus on food ingredients alone, it made it clear that the previously key business of sugar refinement would not be part of the future journey (Yetton et al. 2013). Instead, growth would be related to Danisco business in enzymes, cultures, and textures. Naturally, updated as-is descriptions would be more relevant in these areas.

The other starting point for business case estimates are the assumptions of the businesses targeted. Capability maps provide great templates to reason about the expectations about the target. On one hand, capability maps can be seen as representations of the collective emergent understanding of the target. They become the place where different pieces of information are puzzled together in a way that shows missing, contradictory, and questionable information.

Based on these emergent capability maps, it becomes possible to discuss, capability by capability, what would be the synergistic effect of combining them. These effects could be positive or negative, sometimes both at the same time. Take a production capability, for example. A duplicate production capability for reasonably similar products cries for consolidation to reap economies of scale. But what if one of the companies are based on a produce-to-stock and the other on a produce-to-demand operating model? The production to stock is likely to be cheaper per unit produced, so moving all production to this model will lead to both efficiency improvements and economies of scale. Yet, the negative effects of reduced agility and missed market opportunities at the previously produce-to-demand company may vastly overshadow these benefits.

One company that has been using EA in this way to create to-be and as-is scenarios as the basis for business case development is the US industry consortium Friedkin, which has a business portfolio that ranges from car dealerships to luxury resorts. At Friedkin, acquisitions are driven by the strategic intent to move the business in a certain direction. EA's role is to articulate this intention in the form of a to-be scenario, and the as-is scenarios of both acquirer and acquisition target as the basis for decision-making.

Having a reasonably updated as-is description of the company is a prerequisite for this role of EA. Although not perfect in every detail, this description gives Friedkin the ability to use the strategic intent behind the acquisition to identify which of its business capabilities are at play. With this as a basis, the general overview of the to-be scenario maps both the business capabilities that exists pre-acquisition in Friedkin and the ones that have to be created as part of the acquisition to compete. While Friedkin aims at keeping a reasonably updated general documentation of its as-is architecture, the zooming in on specific business capabilities may require some updates of these capabilities to ensure that the as-is description is of the quality required when these capabilities come into play. Having the high-level business capabilities laid out, Friedkin then maps the underlying capabilities in the operational, information, and technology layers that would support these business capabilities. This forms the to-be scenario for the relevant acquisition, where capabilities are expressed along with tags indicating if they already exist or have to be obtained in relation to the acquisition.

With this baseline, Friedkin can then map potential targets as as-is scenarios. This process is typically relatively similar to mapping of one's own company, with the obvious restriction of information access. However, the as-is model of the acquirer indicates how well the target holds up to the intended to-be scenario. The fit is never perfect. Typically, some capabilities will be missing. These have to be built in the event of a deal. Other capabilities of the target will not fit into the to-be scenario, and will have to be commissioned. With these drawings, Friedkin can reason about the business case associated with one particular acquisition target being clear about what the acquisition can contribute and what it cannot.

Capability models will not give the results of the equation that make the business case, but it will show what is in the equation. Capability models make it possible to espouse knowledge and assumptions. In some cases, legal or strategic restrictions limit the opportunities to verify these assumptions. In other cases, information is available to verify the assumptions during the due diligence exercise. In any case, capability models provide a good overview of what is known to make a better and more informed estimate as to the uncertainties involved in that exercise.

Transformation Needs Assessment

Another critical aspect of selecting a target is to understand what it will take to bring the companies together to realize the synergistic effects. In the case of the acquisition in the oil and gas industry that was discussed above, it would have been critical to assess what work was needed to be done in the 18 months preceding the acquisition to please Wall street. In another acquisition, made by the world's largest shipping line, Maersk Line, in its acquisition of Dutch-British P&O Nedlloyd, the transformation need was severely underestimated (Financial Times 2007). On the surface, it looked like an ideal setup to consolidate two relatively similar operations in the container shipping business. Together, the combined business would have a global market share in the range of 25% with the lowest cost of operation in the industry. However, the combined operation required significant transformation in the operational technology supporting the business.

For example, Maersk Line's supporting IT platform was designed to support a set of local businesses, not global business processes. P&O Nedlloyd on the other hand had an IT platform supporting global processes, but it could not effectively scale to the volumes of the combined businesses. Therefore, the transformational needs in this specific acquisition included the implementation of a brand-new IT platform to support both organizations. This platform was on its way, being configured as Maersk Line contemplated the acquisition. But the platform was delayed and not implemented before the integration work was to start. Clearly a substantial transformation was to be taken into consideration when determining the cost and time required to transform.

No unit is better suited than the EA team to carry out an assessment of the costs associated with implementing the required business and technology transformations to integrate two organizations. EA is all about orchestrating the ongoing transformation of a company. In an advanced capability, EA becomes the nexus through which all organizational transformation activities are channeled. Therefore, enterprise architects know the verticals they are responsible for inside and out, not only on a high level as generic capabilities on a map, but on a more granular level what capacities they have and do not have. They know if they are flexible and can accommodate different processes, support scaling, or can easily be substituted.

At Friedkin, the US consortium introduced above, the transformation needs assessment starts with the capabilities in the to-be scenarios that are tagged as new compared to Friedkin's as-is scenario. For all these operational, information, and technology capabilities, Friedkin investigates if they exist in the acquired company. If they do exist, investigation begins on how to port them onto Friedkin's preexisting capabilities. If they do not exist, these capabilities are marked as transformation gaps. For capabilities that do exist, subsequent analysis includes general capacity constraints as well as adherence to Friedkin's architectural principles. Using the technology architecture, Friedkin understands whether the application in the acquired company can work with Friedkin's application collaboration platform, can be integrated into its security model, introduces more data than can be handled by existing databases, can be hosted on the existing technology stack, etc. Each inconsistency is marked as a transformation gap.

With a basis in the possibly long list of gaps, Friedkin then starts to anticipate the work required to close them:

- Human resources (salaries and individuals with specific competences)
- Financial recourses (without human costs)
- Time requirements

Because of the nature of acquisitions where most of the cost is paid upfront and revenues only collected after integration is done, the time dimension of the transformation needed is critical. Beyond the number of hours of work that each gap requires, time to gap closure is also impacted by bottlenecks in competences, capacities, and the need to sequence work rather than do it in parallel. Although not much of a concern, availability of technical hardware and infrastructure might still be an issue on rare occasions.

Projecting human, financial, and time input needed to address gaps will doubtlessly involve a number of estimates that are based on judgment. Individual architects working in an advanced EA capability would also have good insights in their own IT development organizations' capacities to deliver transformation. If the capability roadmaps are already set where it occupies the full capacity of the development organization, the question arises whether the acquirer wants to push the acquisition integration expectation or to reprioritize. Regardless of the choice, EA is appropriately situated to raise the flag of this need to senior management, whose job it is to make such prioritizations.

Identification of Roadblocks

Roadblocks are specific integration challenges that may turn out so difficult to address that the whole acquisition deal could be questioned. Roadblocks are typically possible to address, but the nature of acquisitions where the cost is taken upfront and rewards are generated incrementally as synergies are realized, makes time-to-synergy a critical factor. Thus, if one or a few specific elements push the time-to-synergy substantially, then that specific issue may present a roadblock in the deal.

If you remember our earlier example of Maersk Line, the need to develop a new IT platform at Maersk Line was probably just the type of roadblock that should have stopped or at least postponed the deal until Maersk Line was ready to acquire. Another example of a roadblock that should have been considered was the product portfolio when one large consumer bank acquired the regional business on one continent from another large consumer bank. Here, the acquired unit offered a range of products that the acquiring bank did not have the technical or operational infrastructure to support. As the acquisition was carved out from the mother company, none of the supporting capabilities followed in the deal. Hence, before the customers of the acquired company could be ported to the acquirer, the acquirer needed to rebuild capabilities at the technical, systems, and operational level. Obviously, this need pushed the integration back years and caused enormous frustration within the staff of the acquirer, who got burnt out one after the other. Overall, although no figures of the deal were ever disclosed, it's not likely the net present value of the investment in the acquisition would ever be positive with such a delay.

A transformation needs assessment is a great starting point to identify roadblocks, but these key issues need particular attention. Such analysis would include a critical reflection of what the assumptions are and what is actually known about the acquirer. One merit of using capability models as the basis for business case estimation is that they reveal what is known and what are just assumptions. For example, take the case where a company that produces mechanical parts to the automotive industry wants to better use spare capacity in its factories by acquiring a smaller competitor and consolidating the production. A capability model can reveal the information pieces that links to this particular capability. Does the acquirer really know what the production capacity in the target looks like? If there are five post-it notes on the wall giving clues about the production process, chances are that the process is reasonably well known as a basis for decision. If there is no actual evidence pointing in any direction, it is a risky move to use an assumption as the basis for a decision that could come to cause much economic damage and potentially crush the careers of people involved.

As a rule of thumb, a roadblock of importance is typically discernable when something new needs to be built to substantiate synergies. Building simply takes much longer than redeploying capabilities. So, in the analysis of roadblocks the EA team would use capability maps to create heat maps over areas where delays would significantly impact synergy realization.

Reverse Integration Potential

Now and then an acquisition has more to offer than at first sight. There might be more of value in a company than the grand strategic plan indicates as the major benefit. Perhaps the sales team is relatively more successful than the acquirer's, or the inventory is small, but order fulfillment is still better, or a certain branch of product development is more efficient so the organization delivers one successful product after the other. These capabilities would be good to preserve post-acquisition, even though they may not be deal breakers. But the question is can you take that single business capability and port it onto the extant enabling capability, or will doing so erase its uniqueness?

Other times, acquisitions are primarily driven by some specific capacity of the acquired company that should be ported to the acquirer and thereby be better utilized than as a stand-alone asset. Such acquisitions are extremely common in the high-tech industries, where companies compete on innovative features in their offerings, but they are also becoming increasingly prominent in industries such as finance, automotive, and healthcare. Commonly, these acquisitions address some innovative business capability that is enabled by operational, systems, and technology capabilities. Therefore, here too the question when assessing if a superior business capability can be ported into the acquiring organization is if it can be supported by the extant set of enabling capabilities in the acquirer, or whether the acquisition's associated capabilities can be incorporated along with the business capabilities.

For example, when Danisco, the Danish industry conglomerate moved to a business focused on food ingredients, acquired the US-based company Genencor for its food culture business (Henningsson 2016). The main synergies anticipated were in increased revenues through cross-selling and a better utilization of the distribution organization. But after the deal, when Danisco started to look into Genencor, it had to admit that its supply chain management capability was more advanced than the one Danisco already had. All key performance indicators that Danisco used for its supply chain looked better in Genencor. This was something that the managers and employees in Genencor became relatively outspoken about. Danisco therefore started to look into whether the same capability could be reverse-integrated as the new global standard in Danisco. At first it looked at the operational capabilities: could it be transformed to work in this way? Could people work according to the new processes for the other products Danisco could offer? Danisco could not see any serious threats here. Individuals would need a bit of training, but they would cope.

System wise, the issue was more difficult. The existing supply chain management system in Danisco would not support the new way of working. Danisco then investigated if they could port Genencor's supply chain management system onto its technological platform. The problem was that Genencor based its supply chain on a system component that was from another technology service provider and could not run efficiently on the same enabling technological infrastructure. There was consequently a barrier for reverse integration of the supply chain management capability that had to be considered in the acquisition. Eventually, sometime after the acquisition and after further consideration it was decided that Danisco would rebuild the system and operational capacities to mirror the ones of Genencor. The cost of doing so was reasonably high, so it was not sure that it contributed positively to the deal value, but was motivated by the fact that otherwise employees in Genencor would be left with the feeling that the unit went backwards in operational efficiency as a consequence of the acquisition. A new system implementation was a low cost compared to that potential outcome, and the supply chain did become more efficient afterwards.

Danisco did not use EA to assess the reverse integration potential, but managed anyway. Clearly, such assessments can be made without EA—at least after the deal, when integration planning typically triggers questions about which capability and which system is the better one. Commonly, to avoid political discussions and to avoid a stagnant process, the acquirer will decide as general rule that its system and its capabilities will be used. This is also the safe solution to avoid technological complexity. But the risk is of course that great business capabilities will be foregone.

Having EA actively engaged in the selection process allows for addressing integration on a more granular level, actively working with the question of great capabilities in the target can be worth redeploying in the acquirer through reverse integration. This would always be an option through completely rebuilding a mirror image of a capability, but it may be more resource demanding than the gains it motivates. And, if the capability that has to be rebuilt was the primary subject for the acquisition, then maybe the acquisition should not be done in the first place.

Suite Analysis

The task of suite analysis applies to companies where the offering is completely or partially digital. Digital products have a unique characteristic in that they are more valuable to customers when they come in integrated suites than as stand-alone products. For instance, a word processing software is more useful in an office suite where content can be imported and exported to other office software, than as a stand-alone software. Theoretically, this is explained in the academic literature with something called the theory of complementarity. In short, digital technologies that complement each other are easier to produce and provide users with more value than technologies that do not complement each other.

For companies with purely digital products, such as software companies, the question of product integration is core to the acquisition value proposal. For SAP, acquiring another software provider means that they can preintegrate the products and make life easier for their customers. This was one of the rationales behind SAP's acquisition of Hybris, an e-commerce provider used by many of SAP's customers to complement the SAP suite (Henningsson et al. 2016).

As a result of the process of digitalization more and more companies are experiencing that what they offer contains some digital element. In consequence, they also need to consider how the products can form suites, as their customers will ask for using them in this way. Integration of the digital product element is one way to create value through the acquisition.

Investigating the potential for developing suites of products post-acquisition is a suitable task for the EA team. General managers of a traditional manufacturing, finance, or automotive organization cannot be expected to judge the technological difficulties of suiting products. Given its unique understanding of how technological and organizational resources can be bundled, the EA team can effectively assume the responsibility to ensure that the target's IT-based offerings can be integrated and coexist with acquirers' existing suite of products.

Platform Consistency Modelling

An activity that is uniquely relevant to acquisitions of divestments is platform consistency modelling. In a divestment to acquisition transaction, the vendor typically sells of one of its business units to another multibusiness organization. The assumption in this transaction is that the new owner will have a "parenting advantage," meaning that the business unit for some reason is better off with the new owner. Such reasons could include available funds for continued growth, more know-how about the industry in which the business unit operates, or access to a wider and more relevant sales network. Some of these reasons would be synergy based and dependent on integration. This should be treated as any other type of synergy in the activities above. But, regardless of the underlying reasons, the sheer fact that the business unit is moving from one parenting company to another could create a particular challenge that EA is very well situated to detect. This is the issue that pre-acquisition the business unit is operating on a broader, more comprehensive IT enablement provided by the parent company. For example, if the vendor has a supply chain capability as part of the corporate capabilities, and the acquirer has not, this could mean that there is platform inconsistency that somehow has to be dealt with (see Fig. 5.2).

This was the case when two consumer bank's made a deal that involved the transfer of a regional business from one bank to the other. The divesting bank wanted to exit a particular geographical region to focus on its home market. Before the divestment the regional unit had been extensively supported by the vendor's global IT platform. Beyond capabilities such as customer management and financial reporting, the corporate platform also enabled globally valid products such as credit cards. The acquirer had its own global IT platform, but it did not support exactly the same products. For example, the credit card was not supported by the acquirer's IT platform. Here was a platform inconsistency that enterprise architects could have acknowledged if included in the acquisition selection. In this particular case, they

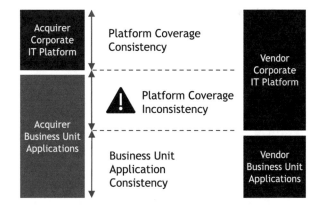

Fig. 5.2 Platform consistency between acquirer and vendor in a divest to acquisition transaction

were not included and the consequence was that this inconsistency went unnoticed until after the transaction contract had been signed.

Identification of Nontransferable Enablers

The reason that the IT-enablement of the credit card product in the example above was not included in the divestment to acquisition transaction was because components of IT platforms are typically not easily transformed to another platform. The vendor had little possibility to carve this particular piece out and transfer it. IT platforms are not portfolios of different applications that can be moved around, so platform inconsistencies are in a sense one example of a nontransferable enabler, but there are also other reasons why enablers cannot be transferred. These include license issues, competition barriers, or that other business units in the vendor are using the same IT enablers. Regardless, nontransferable enablers are an issue that needs proper attention in the acquisitions of divestments, and here EA can help.

If deal-making managers spot potential issues in the target considered, they should approach EA to make an assessment of the situation. The starting point to identify nontransferable enablers are a profound understanding of the enablers that the acquirer already possesses. If these can be reused, the problem is probably not that bad and should not be a major concern in the selection of an acquisition. But, if the acquirer has no counterpart enabler, determining what to do with the nontransferable enabler needs to form part of the contract negotiation. Transition service agreements are an option, but these are technically complex and costly. Procuring and implementing new technological enablers is another option, but this is costly and time consuming. Bridging the potential gap could imply significant cost on and problems for one of the parties in the deal, and should be factored into the sales price.

Chapter Key Points

- An advanced EA capability can effectively ease the challenge of estimating the actual value of the target for a specific acquirer.
- EA holds the ability to forecast complementary aspects between two organizations at the capability level.
- In the selection phase of acquisition, EA can contribute to:
  - *Business case estimation* through the use of EA artifacts that help to determine the capabilities in place to support the new business and the need for stand-alone capabilities
  - *Transformation needs assessment* by estimation cost for the transformation needed to leverage potential synergistic effects

- *Roadblock analysis* by verification of the possibility to retain separate business capabilities, while still redeploying existing operational, systems, and technical capabilities
- *Discovery of reverse integration potential* by exposing the possibility to redeploy capabilities from the target in the acquirer
- *Suite analysis* by investigating if the target's digital offerings contribute to the suite of integrated offerings in the acquirer
- *Platform consistency modelling* that allows early discovery of gaps in the IT enablement of a target that is acquired as a divestment
- *Identification of nontransferable enablers* for which transition agreements may be needed

References

Financial Times. (2007). *New Maersk chief makes shipping line 'top priority'*. Accessed October 28, 2019, from https://www.ft.com/content/b4de0b2e-8bdd-11dc-af4d-0000779fd2ac

Henningsson, S. (2016). The acquisition IT integration challenge: Danisco/DuPont. In N. B. Andersen (Ed.), *Cases on IT leadership* (pp. 123–142). Copenhagen: Samfundslitteratur.

Henningsson, S., Kude, T., & Popp, K. M. (2016). Managing the technology acquisition integration paradox at SAP. In *The 37th International Conference on Information Systems*, Dublin, Ireland. Association for Information Systems, AIS Electronic Library (AISeL).

Yetton, P., Henningsson, S., & Bjorn-Andersen, N. (2013). Ready to Acquire': IT resources for a growth-by-acquisition strategy. *MIS Quarterly Executive, 12*(1), 19–35.

Chapter 6
Integration: *Direct* Work Streams

If the selection phase is where *potential* value creation is identified, then the integration phase is where value creation *happens*. A large amount of research points to the integration phase as where most acquisitions go wrong. People, cultures, processes, strategies, and technologies need to blend together into a whole that forms something greater than its parts, i.e. something that enables the strategic rationale motivating the acquisition, without compromising the long-term coherence of the organization and do so without disrupting business, damaging operational capacity, and scaring away customers. Many times, different benefits are mutually excluding, leading to priorities that at best are semirational, and at worst nasty political struggles.

When the Commonwealth Bank of Australia acquired the State Bank of Victoria, there were dual business benefits in, on one hand, the economies of scale to be realized in consolidation of the retail bank operation, but also possibilities for the acquirer to improve its business in the private wealth management domain where the acquisition had a superior business (Johnston and Yetton 1996). Figuring out which systems to keep and which IT team should be in charge of what component became a political haggle, fueled by the traditional tension between Sydney and Melbourne in which the respective companies' headquarters were located.

An acquisition integration project will never be perfect. It is in the very nature of acquisitions that some things will be paradoxical and mutually excluding. It is also inherent in its complex nature that unexpected things will happen. A recent research review we conducted showed that there are at least 190 different factors influencing the outcome of the IT integration project in acquisitions (Henningsson et al. 2018). Some are more or less outside the control of the acquirer, including vendor actions in divestment acquisitions and transforming market conditions. Many of these factors work in systems with other factors, and only have an important impact when a range of conditions materializes at the same time. Because of its complexity, it is very unlikely that the acquirer has thought of exactly everything and made a correct assessment of all possible implications. If no changes are made to the integration

© Springer Nature Switzerland AG 2020
S. Henningsson, G. N. Toppenberg, *Architecting Growth in the Digital Era*,
https://doi.org/10.1007/978-3-030-39482-0_6

plan, it is probably because the acquirer was inflexible enough to not recognize the need, rather than that there was no need to do it.

Recognizing that acquisition integration is the equivalent of open-heart surgery while the patient is running a marathon, it would be naïve to think that EA would solve all acquisition integration challenges. This will not happen. Effective integration requires that the acquirer masters a long list of disciplines. Nevertheless, what EA uniquely can bring to the table in the integration phase is a mechanism for reasoning around what needs to be prioritized and how work fits into a broader transformational context. Specifically, EA can in the integration phase provide:

- Exposure of conflicts in aspirations and fixing priorities
- Improved resource reutilization and minimize redevelopment
- Integration work aligned with the general transformation process

To do this, EA contributes to five tasks: *complete to-be state definition, organizational design, IT enablement, roadmap development,* and *carve-out bridging* (Table 6.1). The commensurability between these tasks is that they all take the EA models produced in the selection phase as the starting point and evolve them further.

Table 6.1 EA in the acquisition integration

EA activity	Purpose	Critical accomplishments
To-be state definition	Identification of "integration debt" for specific solutions, development of operational scenarios, and target state for business, operations, systems, and technology views	Development of operational scenarios and target state for business, operations, systems, and technology views. The EA team maps the current technical capabilities of both acquirer and target's state for the integration.
Organizational design	Alignment of acquired entity's resource models and organizational models	The acquisition team utilizes the reference models to determine the conceptual integration of the workforce into the workforce model.
IT enablement	Site and infrastructure technology enablement	The technology models contained in the reference model are used to determine the needed transformation to support the systems and operational capabilities needed to support the target's business capabilities.
Roadmap development	Capability integration roadmap, migration model development	The EA team leverages the to-be scenario capability maps and transformation needs assessment to model required changes to each capability that requires transformation and incorporate the changes into capability roadmaps for the coming 18 months.
Carve-out bridging	Alternatives for bridging enablement gaps of divestment acquisitions	EA is positioned to identify options and suggest preferences for bridging gaps in the enablement of divestment acquisitions

Models inherited from the selection phase would be focused on the most significant areas during the rush of the due diligence, and be prone to assumptions that have not been possible to verify. In the integration phase, EA evolves them into blueprints of sufficient detail that makes them actionable.

In acquisitions where EA is only involved post deal, when the task of "making things work" lands in the laps of the integration team, then several of the architect's tasks would be similar, at the start, to what was described above when discussing EA in the selection phase. There are obvious reasons as to why this work identifying the value potential of the acquisition should be done before signing the contract. But, if this is not done, the starting point of the integration should be the development of capability maps showing the as-is and to-be scenarios, and likely the transformation will need assessment.

In acquisitions that are divestments by other organizations, EA would need to break out from the boundaries of the own organization, because orchestrating the transformation of the transaction is an activity that transcends organizational boundaries. The exposure of conflicts, optimization of resource utilization and organization of task dependencies is a job that evolves the EA function of the vendor's organization, if one exists. If not, EA will have to find another counterpart to interact with, because the job still needs to be done.

Refined To-Be State Definition

The to-be state models developed in the selection phase are typically subject to two limitations. One is that they typically limited in coverage to particular key areas. The other is that they commonly are based on assumptions rather than validated facts. Expanding the coverage of capability models should at this stage be a reasonably straightforward task for an experienced EA team, as the activity resembles any capability model activity. The extent of the task can also be eased if the acquired company has a good EA practice itself or at least documentation of its system and technology landscape. However, many times this is not the case. Maintaining a good EA practice is an investment that has long-term positive implications on the balance sheet. Companies and business units that are likely to be sold off are prone to focus investments on activities with more immediate effects. Reducing the EA function is one of these moves that can bring up profit momentarily to stage a unit for acquisition. Therefore, extant documentation of the target's EA needs to be dealt with as assumptions that need to be verified.

Another set of assumptions is inherited from the parts of the capability models that could not be verified in the due diligence, because of confidentiality reasons or simply time constraints. It is important here that the task of tagging of capabilities in the initial models were done correctly so that assumptions are not taken as facts in this stage. It also helps if the same individuals can prolong their engagement with the tasks, as "assumption" in reality is not a binary tag. Some areas tagged as assumptions may be plausible while others simply have been left without consideration. Knowledge at this level of detail will be difficult to carry through in written documentation.

Another advantage of having the same architects continue to work with the refined to-be state definition is that over time, this engagement on both sides of the deal will inform the architects what issues are materializing on the post-deal side that should have been identified already in the pre-deal stage. Anyone who only works on the pre-deal side of the acquisition is less likely to understand the impact of the pre-deal work than someone who personally experiences the merits of the work in the post-deal phases. This includes enterprise architects who hand over initial models and do not experience how they are later used.

Organizational Design

Following the to-be state definition, EA can contribute to organizational design, in which the distribution of the acquired workforce is decided. The organizational design is about how the business and operational capabilities are translated to people actively doing their jobs. How are they grouped into teams and placed into organizational entities? Where should they be located? Who should be in the teams to make them function effectively? These are among the critical questions that have to be resolved to actually deliver the organizational capabilities that enable a business to prosper.

To do this, the acquisition team utilizes organizational capability models provided by EA to determine the conceptual integration of the workforce into the workforce model. Here, EA would not be the principal driver of the activity, but will contribute by providing the right models, as well as actively engage in the use of this model.

Including EA in the organizational design enables a business-centric point of entry to the organizational design, rather than a resource-centric starting point. One way to approach the distribution of workforce is to assume that everyone would be doing more or less the same thing after the deal and do a functional merger of the workforce. This means that individuals who worked in product development would be merged into a shared product development organization, and individuals who worked with supply chain management would be located into the supply chain management organization. The functional manager is tasked with the job to "right-size" the function given the budget. Then, if the units become too big, individuals from the acquisitions are made redundant. While this is one possible way of working, it may lead to unnecessary negative effects for the individuals and create difficult gaps elsewhere in the organization.

Using capability maps as the starting point for the organizational design enables a more holistic approach to how operational capabilities are delivered. Working on the overall level gives greater possibilities to fit in individuals that can work in several capabilities regardless of where they organizationally were placed before the acquisition. A project leader in product development may, for example be assigned project leader duties in relation to other organizational capabilities. The functional lead would not know about this need in another part of the organization. It is also easier to keep teams intact and preserve those constellations that are working effectively together.

Capability models also give an opportunity to identify gaps that exist in the organizational design. An acquisition creates new possibilities that require new capabilities and give additional weight to some other capabilities. Taking the product development capability again as an example, even if both acquirer and target have such a capability it may not mean that they are similar and should be combined. In an acquisition within the manufacturing industry, for instance, the acquirer's product development capability may be dedicated the task of configuring and packaging components as complete solutions to the company's customers. In contrast, the acquired company's product development capability may work with the materials going into the products. If the latter was not deemed a focus of the combined organization and this second product development capability was discontinued, as the profiles of the staff in the discontinued unit do not match the acquirer's need for product developers, the individuals will regrettably be made redundant in order to optimize the new organization.

In the organizational design, the capability maps consist a starting point, but they cannot be used without the active involvement of the architect that created them. The enterprise architects that have produced and managed capability maps would typically have an understanding of the people, skills, and processes that enable a capability (Fig. 6.1). Take the example of an acquirer that wants to consolidate the product development capability in relation to an acquisition. Looking at the capability map will tell very little about what the individuals would need to do and therefore what to look for in the individuals. Enterprise architects working at the organizational and business level of the company should know not only that the capabilities exist, but also what they actually deliver and how they are working. This knowledge is a prerequisite for using the maps correctly.

IT Enablement

Once the organizational design is concluded, the next task that EA can contribute to is the design of the IT enablement of this organization, which is how the technological resources can support the organizational design efficiently. Once again, the

Fig. 6.1 Enterprise architect's extended understanding of capabilities

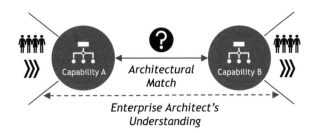

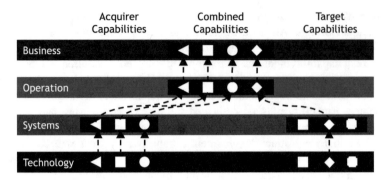

Fig. 6.2 IT enablement of operational capabilities

capability models for the affected areas form the starting point to drill down into the capacities of extant technologies.

The IT enablement is an investigation of which technological resources from the two merging companies should support the operational capabilities (Fig. 6.2). Here, including EA in this activity enables a process that takes its starting point in what the organization should be delivering and extends that to the inquiry of what is the most effective technological support. In practice, this involves a comparison of the acquirer's and acquisition's systems and technology resources to analyze what they can deliver and how they could combine.

In this general task, an enterprise architect can be tasked to investigate which adjustments are needed to systems and technical capabilities to support the added operations. For example, in a US acquisition in the software industry, the enterprise architect discovered that a minor extension of a product database was required to support the acquired business product catalogue and that an extension of the technical infrastructure were required to support the new geographical locations added by the acquired unit. These additions were added to the IT integration workstream.

Minor adjustments in technology are to be expected in any acquisition, although sometimes more extensive modifications are needed, like when Maersk Line acquired P&O Nedlloyd and needed to rebuild its core enterprise system. Even in horizontal acquisitions where a company buys one of its similar-looking competitors there will typically be a few new products to be accommodated in the project database, some new production, warehouse or development locations to be supported, local legislation that needs to be considered, or partner connections to be established.

EA's role in the IT enablement is not only to take part in the functional analysis of IT resources, but also analyze to which extent they conform to the acquirer's architectural principles. It may be that the acquirer's resources deliver a function that is superior to what the acquirer already possesses, but if that functionality comes with a deviation from the architectural principles, it should be marked as a deviation that needs to be considered in the transformation roadmap so as to not comprise the long-term viability of the IT platform.

Roadmap Development

The roadmap development is the task of making integration work meld together with other ongoing transformations in the acquirer, so as to make the best use of resources, reduce operational disruption to a minimum, and make the company evolve as a coherent whole.

In practice, an advanced EA capability would orchestrate the ongoing transformation of the company through capability roadmaps that captures a migration model to realize the to-be state. Here, the EA team leverages a capability integration roadmap showing the capabilities to map systems and technologies and determine the relative difficulty of integration and the options to consider along with a cost estimate. The different deadlines of the integration project, typically articulated as Day 1, Day 30, Day 90, and Day 180+ milestones, should feed into the relevant planning cycle for the ongoing organizational transformation (Fig. 6.3). Of course, this is more valid for minor acquisitions or when the acquirer handles several acquisitions at the time. In the case of a larger acquisition, it is more common that the integration work becomes the single transformation stream until major synergy targets have been met.

Roadmapping the capability transformation is important for at least two reasons. One is that it exposes the need to make priorities for what change is more important than the other. Frequently, the answer is that acquisition integration is more important than everything else. At Danske Bank, for instance, acquisitions always meant that all other changes to the technological landscape were to be put on hold until the acquired bank had been effectively integrated into the shared platform. This was partly to avoid "integration into a running target," but partly also because the acquisition IT integration project consumed all available IT resources for 12–18 months.

In the acquisition of the Canadian company SMITH Commerce server by the Danish omni-channel solutions company Sitecore, the capability roadmaps

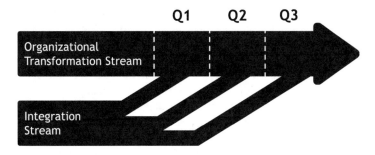

Fig. 6.3 Orchestration of organizational transformation and integration work streams

developed for the integration were used as a basis to understand the need to postpone integration (Henningsson and Nishu 2019). This was because Sitecore needed the IT development team that was best suited for the integration on a different project together with Microsoft. Sitecore considered the options, including engaging another development team to do the task, but eventually decided that the most reasonable thing to do was to delay the integration by 6 months.

These two examples—Sitecore and Danske Bank—show that the work of each capability in capability roadmaps with assigned development resources will effectively convey the speed by which the development organization can deliver.

The other reason capability roadmaps are effective to orchestrate the integration work is because acquisition-integration-related changes can be coordinated with changes in the capability for other reasons. It can be that the capability is to be upgraded for some entirely different reason. In one acquisition we studied, the EA teams were just about to adjust the capability roadmaps for the affected capabilities to reflect the changes in IT enablement when the architects identified that the whole IT infrastructure in this specific business area was soon to undergo a major update. This was shown in the capability roadmaps that the acquirer maintained. With this knowledge, the acquisition integration team decided to postpone the required changes to the IT infrastructure required by the acquisition until after the infrastructure project was finished. Not only did this lead to that work only being done once, but it also minimized the operational disruption to the business unit.

Carve-Out Bridging

A key dilemma in a divestment to acquisition transaction is, as explained earlier, that often there is a gap in the technological enablement of the transferred business unit. This means that if the vendor only cuts off and transfers what is uniquely associated with the divested unit, there is a gap to fill through a bridging process. EA can assist here by detailing what the gap looks like and what are the options to fill it. There are several possibilities to temporarily fill a technology enablement gap, which could be needed in the short run but not effective in the long. From the vendor's side, a gap can be filled by system transfer, system replication, and through transitional service provision. In the system transfer, the vendor actually takes on the job to carefully separate a tightly coupled application from its IT landscape to be able to ship it with the acquirer. This can be a good choice even if part of the vendor's remaining business still uses this application, as it gives the vendor the possibility to procure a solution that is most suitable to the remaining users rather than furthering the use of a partially stranded asset. In the replication operation, the vendor retains its version of an application, but seeks to logically separate the data going into the application before a version of it is transferred to the acquirer. In the transitional service provisioning, the vendor agrees to support the divested unit for a limited amount of time, enabling the acquirer to enact on different long-term possibilities. A typical transition contract would last for 3–6 months, but some may drag out for several years.

From the acquirer's side, a carve-out gap can be bridged by temporarily hosting an acquired unit on another business unit's related application. One issue with this is that the IT enablement may not be suitable for its new use. For example, an order system may not support well the sales processes of the acquired unit and a product planning system can lead to suboptimal planning. The risk is of course that the unsuitable arrangement becomes permanent and results in inefficient operation and IT complexities.

Finally, with the proliferation of cloud services, acquirers now have increasing possibilities to "park" an acquisition in a solution of standardized, nonintegrated cloud services until its clear what the long-term solution should become. Some of the cloud services could become permanent solutions, where others are retired when the acquirer manages to provide solutions that are more integrated with the rest of the IT landscape.

EA is a critical tool to discover these possibilities, and can contribute to determining the shortest route to fill the gap. This includes gauging the long-term implications on flexibility by co-using technological capabilities across business units, or pinpointing to when questions need to be asked about the security concerns in relation to cloud technologies. Maybe the replication of system at the vendor is outside the scope of the transaction contract, but still something that should be negotiated because the only viable alternative is to start a sourcing process to implement the equivalent. Sometimes there are only poor options on the table, but at least with the help of EA decision-makers one can have all options and their consequences on the table when making decisions about how to bridge the carve-out gap.

Chapter Key Points

- Acquisition integration is the equivalent to open-heart surgery while the patient is running a marathon and as a result EA will never solve all acquisition integration challenges.
- What EA uniquely brings to the integration phase is a platform for reasoning around what needs to be prioritized and how work can fit into a broader transformational context.
- In the integration phase, EA can contribute to:
  - *To-be state definition* by development of capability maps for target state scenarios
  - *Organizational design* utilizing reference models to determine the integration of the workforce
  - *IT enablement* by using technological models to determine the needed transformation of systems and operational capabilities
  - *Roadmap development* leveraging to-be scenarios and transformation needs models to develop capability roadmaps
  - *Carve-out bridging* by identify alternatives and suggesting preferences to cover gaps in the enablement of divestment acquisitions

References

Henningsson, S., & Nishu, N. (2019). Sitecore: Retaining technological leadership through digital tech acquisitions. In N. Urbach & M. Röglinger (Eds.), *Digitalization cases* (pp. 183–204). Cham: Springer.

Henningsson, S., Yetton, P. W., & Wynne, P. J. (2018). A review of information system integration in mergers and acquisitions. *Journal of Information Technology, 33*(4), 255–303.

Johnston, K. D., & Yetton, P. W. (1996). Integrating information technology divisions in a bank merger fit, compatibility and models of change. *The Journal of Strategic Information Systems, 5*(3), 189–211.

Chapter 7
Continuation: *Monitoring* Progression

Just because the acquisition project is finished, it does not mean the work is over quite yet. In the postintegration continuation phase, the retrospective work to evaluate actions and their outcomes as well as preparing for the next challenge begins. This is a challenge that is relevant for all acquirers, as the long-term effect of acquisitions have implications for innovation potential and organizational agility, but the challenge is particularly relevant for acquirers that repeatedly engage in acquisitions as in this case the effects of each acquisition will cumulate over time.

One could expect that acquirers that make multiple acquisitions, so-called serial acquirers, over time will improve in their acquisition capabilities and generate more value from acquisitions than their peers. The correlation between the number of acquisitions and performance is, however, not so strong. Indeed, some companies, such as Cisco, CEMEX, and Siemens, that are notorious serial acquirers have developed acquisition capabilities with reliable performance that gives them an edge over their competitors. But for companies that make a handful of acquisitions, the performance of the second, third, and fourth acquisition is too often *declining*, regardless of whether performance is measured through shareholder value, short-term acquisition benefits, or long-term operational performance (Barkema and Schijven 2008b).

There are two explanations for this surprising pattern. The first has to do with the difficulties to draw learning from one acquisition to the next (Barkema and Schijven 2008a). This is partly because it is difficult to judge the outcome of an acquisition project as good or bad. As explained in Chap. 2, the outcome of acquisitions can be defined in so many ways that an acquisition will typically have elements of both. In addition, it is very difficult to judge what led to the outcome in the first place. Was the result achieved *because of* or *despite* the communication in the project? Could another way of organizing the due diligence have spotted *more* of the latent challenges, or would it have uncovered *less* of the issues? Because all acquisitions are to some degree unique there are no reference points to compare results with. The ambiguity of acquisition outcome in combination with the ambiguity of what

© Springer Nature Switzerland AG 2020
S. Henningsson, G. N. Toppenberg, *Architecting Growth in the Digital Era*,
https://doi.org/10.1007/978-3-030-39482-0_7

Table 7.1 EA in the acquisition continuation

EA activity	Purpose	Critical accomplishments
Integration evaluation	Providing metrics for integration performance evaluation	Based on its ability to overview the acquisition transformation, EA can be tasked with determining the extent to which the key integration measurements have been achieved in the stipulated time frame.
Integration correction	Corrections to ensure that platform integrity was restored	The EA team can be tasked with documenting deviations from the integration plan in the reference model and to plan for corrective action to restore "integration debt" caused during the acquisition process.

actually caused the outcome is referred to as the double ambiguity of acquisitions (Zollo 2009).

The second explanation to why serial acquirers sometimes show declining acquisition performance is because the inefficiencies that accumulate across a series of acquisitions. Any acquisition will leave some residual inefficiencies caused by quick-fixes and suboptimal solutions to meet critical timelines. Over time, these inefficiencies will accumulate and make the acquirer less agile. This hampers not only subsequent acquisitions, but more generally the company's ability to innovate. Therefore, restoring the debt caused by an acquisition is vital both for serial acquirers, and even for companies that do single acquisitions.

EA can contribute to both the evaluation and restoration of debt in the acquisition continuation phase, because of its central position and holistic overview of the ongoing transformation of the company. To do this, EA needs to be engaged in two activities: integration evaluation and integration correction (Table 7.1).

Integration Evaluation

The issue of learning from acquisitions is referred to as "superstitious learning" and attributed to the double ambiguity in complex strategic projects (Zollo 2009). These are in contrast to more routine-like tasks that we encounter in everyday life both at work and at home. Take the challenge of driving from home to work, for example. The first time you do it, you encounter all sorts of issues like congested streets, road work, and lack of parking. Going the same distance every day, you learn when to go, which streets to avoid, and which parking is likely to be available at what time. This is a process of experience accumulation that leads to the establishment of a highly efficient routine for the task of driving from home to work. The learning happens by the testing of different minor variations, where the outcome of each test is immediate and clear.

The sort of learning curve where performance is directly linked to the number of experiences has been found to fit a description of how organizations develop many capabilities, including, for example, the production of goods and services, but they do not work well as an explanation to acquirers' acquisition performance. Researchers disagree whether on average there is a small positive effect of experience, no effect, or even a negative one, but the fact is that many acquirers that attempt a second or third acquisition do experience a decrease in their performance (Barkema and Schijven 2008a). This is so, partly, because they infer the wrong conclusions based on the first experience and incorrectly think that a practice that worked the last time will work equally well the next time.

The effect of superstitious learning has been demonstrated with a simple card game. If someone plays a new game with unfamiliar rules she will rapidly learn how to be successful in this game. If she then plays the same game with a new group that are unfamiliar with the rules, the experienced player will initially be more successful than her peers. But, if the experiment is changed so that the expert and novice player instead play a game with the same basic structure, but with slightly altered rules, the outcome will be different. Then the experienced player performs poorer than the novice players. This is explained by that fact the experienced player will incorrectly assume that the same strategies will hold for the slightly new game. So, in short, when it comes to acquisitions, it is better to have no experience than knowledge based on erroneous assumptions.

Acquisitions seem to follow the same pattern as the card game: they are very prone to erroneous generalizations as the "game" is always shifting from one acquisition to the next. But this problem can be addressed, as it fundamentally is based on a semiautomatic and nonreflective inference of actions and their outcomes. Therefore, the solution is to be found in deliberate evaluation that carefully walks through the actions in the project and revisits their individual effects, as well as how several actions interact to form specific outcomes. The objective of the evaluation is not to arrive at a binary good/bad verdict for each activity, but to foster a greater understanding of cause and outcome among the participants in the project. Evaluation documents will be produced, but are most often retired in a drawer somewhere. Instead, it is the knowledge gained among the participants that lives on and feeds into the next project.

The starting point for any evaluation is the strategic rationale for the acquisition. For example, some may want to rapidly get market access before global patents expire, to gain economies of scale in production, to graft a rapidly growing new business area to the extant business, or to secure access to top talent and world-class teams that cannot be sourced from the market. In each of these acquisitions, the yardstick for success would be extremely different. In one, the time to completion would be critical, but in another, without any relevance. In one, low staff turnover would be the critical achievement, while in another, the objective could be to reduce headcount as much as possible. In yet another acquisition, the target's ability to operate independently after the deal would make or break the value potential, while in the next acquisition, lowered cost from operational synergies would make the deal worthwhile. Regardless of the rationale of the acquisition, these fundamental reasons are what the acquisition project should be held against.

Defining the rationale and the objectives against what an acquisition should be evaluated against is of course beyond the capacities and duties of EA, but EA is

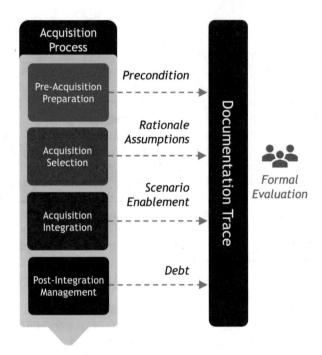

Fig. 7.1 Project documentation trace

particularly well suited to lead the assessment. If EA has been involved as an orchestrating function across the project, it will hold the overarching view of preparation work, key criteria behind the target selection, and priorities in the integration. EA would also have documented the acquisition project over its phases, through capability maps, scenario models, tagged heat maps, roadmaps, and other EA artifacts. This trace of documentation consists the foundation for evaluation as it captures in detail all the activities that have been undertaken in the project (Fig. 7.1).

The use of the project trace is, however, not straightforward for an outsider. On the surface it is a massive amount of documentation produced and if all details where to be addressed in the evaluation, then the acquisition team would not be ready for the next challenge until several years later. The golden balance to strike in the evaluation is to use the trace left by EA to do a formal and structured evaluation that goes beyond just general discussions of what went well and not so well, while still not getting entrenched in details that did not matter for the big picture. Here, the tacit knowledge from having worked with the models is critical to strike this balance. Specifically, a good starting point to direct evaluation work is to use the EA artifacts to rediscover:

- *Key decisions* that were recognized as critical in the process or that were ignored in the process but should have been given proper attention
- *Deviations* in the process, either between or within the different phases:
  - Direction of preparation vs. actual acquisition target
  - Estimated value potential in acquisition selection vs. realized value potential
  - Integration planning vs. integration execution
- *Surprises* along the journey that redirected the acquisition process

In addition, a particular acquisition can benefit from investigation of additional aspects of particular relevance. For example, an acquirer can decide to focus on improving its ability to make correct value potential estimates in the selection phase. With this focus, it would be relevant to evaluate all assumptions made in the selection phase and to track down the extent to which these assumptions were later changed.

Another particular case would be the acquisition made by a novice acquirer, where the acquisition is the first real test if the operational, system, and technology capabilities of the acquirer are flexible enough to support continued growth. In many cases, a company that has been stable over time has focused on building capabilities that are functionally fitted for the job, but not flexible enough to be adapted. Flexibility may not have been a concern when investments where made in the past, and therefore estimates of flexibility have never been done.

Many companies experience their monolith enterprise resource planning systems as concrete when they try to modify them to support new products, services, processes, or locations introduced through the acquisition. As discussed in relation to acquisition preparation, changes of the kind of IT infrastructure preparation is measured in years rather than months. So, if the evaluation concludes that the IT setup is not built for travelling, then aspirations of continued growth should shed light on the need for infrastructural changes as preparation for the next challenge.

Elimination of Integration Debt

The second reason the acquisition performance of serial acquirers often declines over time has to do with the minor inefficiencies that accumulates across a series of acquisitions. Some of these inefficiencies comes from the fact that under the time pressure to rapidly consolidate organizations, managers are often forced to make suboptimal decisions with a short time horizon. Another set of inefficiencies originates in the complexity of acquisition, which makes it impossible to cognitively cover and optimize all details of the project. With several thousands of decisions to make, some will no doubt be less than perfect and should be revisited at a later stage.

Yet another source for introduction of inefficiencies comes from the historical legacy of technology that limits the options to introduce new technologies and to transform operation capabilities. Technological infrastructures are highly path dependent, meaning that past decisions are hard to reverse (because of how they are nestled and embedded into other technologies) and limit future options. For example, when Danisco, the Danish company building a global business in food ingredients through acquisitions, acquired the Finish company Cultor, Danisco was running its business based in 150 relatively independent business units (Henningsson 2016). Each of these units had its own ERP and unique IT setup. When integrating Cultor, Danisco needed to continue the very decentralized IT strategy, even though this was not optimal from the perspective of reaping economies of scale in production and shared distribution network. The integration project took almost 3 years and as a consequence, the IT landscape only grew more complex, making it even harder to work with in the subsequent acquisition.

So, what happened then to Danisco is something that happens to most serial acquirers: Danisco had to put its acquisition program on hold and rebuild the IT platform from scratch, in a more scalable way. IT complexity created a barrier for the growth strategy and something needed to be done. Putting the acquisition program on hold was not the ideal option, but action had to be taken to build in the option of growth into the platform. In this way, Danisco got rid of the accumulated inefficiencies and could start from scratch. Because the platform was designed with the purpose of being scalable, in the continued growth, integration was done in a few months rather than years.

Even more important than enabling growth by acquisition, restoring the IT infrastructure to get rid of the technological debt made it possible for Danisco to innovate faster. A complex, inflexible IT setup limits the innovation options and lowers the ability of the company to respond to environmental changes. With the new IT platform, Danisco could faster move into new markets, roll out new products and dynamically adjust strategies based on learning from the very first day of the move. Importantly, Danisco also defined architectural principles that were to prevent the IT infrastructure growing complex again. The scalable IT infrastructure was defined as a key priority, supported entirely by Danisco's top management. Because Danisco also combined its new scalable IT infrastructure setup with evaluation processes that allowed for learning and improvement, it managed to turn the performance development around. Danisco's capability to acquire went from gradual decay to continuous improvement (Fig. 7.2).

To avoid the accumulation of inefficiencies introduced by acquisitions, EA should be tasked to continuously survey the health of the technology and business capabilities. There are several health metrics that can be used as a general temperature check, including:

- Policies
- Dependencies
- Architectural maturity
- Data quality
- Security

In addition, the EA team can use the original to-be scenarios as blueprints to document variations introduced in the integration process. This comparison between the intended to-be scenario and the as-is reality will capture the inefficiencies also at

Fig. 7.2 Evolution of Danisco's acquisition integration performance (©2019 The Authors, reprinted with permission)

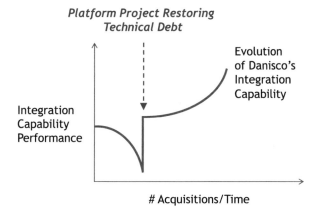

the operational level. Inefficiencies may be of such kind that the go-to-market model has been compromised or that some less effective capability has been introduced because it was the only option not to compromise the technological integrity. Any such deviations need to be recorded and translated into development roadmaps as they consist of apparent possibilities for business improvement that should not be foregone.

So, to bring a close to the acquisition project and move into an operational phase, any deviations from the intended to-be scenario and reduction in the health metrics has to be recoded as organizational and technological debt. It is critical that EA perform this activity, as the end of one acquisition is the starting point of the preparation for the next one. And this logic also holds more broadly for any organizational change. The end of an acquisition project is also the start of preparation for any strategic change project, be it a new market entry, product line, or delivery model. Having done an acquisition should not hamper such moves in the future.

Chapter Key Points

- In the postintegration continuation phase, the retrospective work to evaluate actions and their outcomes as well as preparing for the next challenge starts.
- EA enables evaluation and restoration in the acquisition continuation phase because of its central position and holistic overview of the ongoing transformation of the company.
- In the continuation phase, EA can contribute to:
    - *Integration evaluation* based on its ability to overview the transformation, provide metrics for performance evaluation, and examine if the acquisition holds up to these measurements
    - *Integration correction* by documenting deviations from integration plans and acting to restore technical debt incurred during the integration

References

Barkema, H. G., & Schijven, M. (2008a). How do firms learn to make acquisitions? A review of past research and an agenda for the future. *Journal of Management, 34*(3), 594–634.

Barkema, H. G., & Schijven, M. (2008b). Toward unlocking the full potential of acquisitions: The role of organizational restructuring. *Academy of Management Journal, 51*(4), 696–722.

Henningsson, S. (2016). The acquisition IT integration challenge: Danisco/DuPont. In N. B. Andersen (Ed.), *Cases on IT leadership* (pp. 123–142). Copenhagen: Samfundslitteratur.

Zollo, M. (2009). Superstitious learning with rare strategic decisions: Theory and evidence from corporate acquisitions. *Organization Science, 20*(5), 894–908.

Part III
Back at the Office

In the previous chapters of this book we focused on developing the cognitive keys needed to grasp the full potential of advanced EA capability in the context of an acquisition. We presented the acquisition challenge, explained what characterizes an advanced EA capability, and detailed the use of such capabilities in the different phases of an acquisition project. Taken together, this now gives us a foundation to engage EA in the acquisition process.

Taking on the role of a transformational agent is critical to establishing EA as a contributor to business excellence, but can also be a daunting task. If you have made it to this point in the book and still feel excited about the potential, we are now going to offer you some guidance on how to start the journey of engaging EA in your company's acquisition.

In the three remaining chapters of this book, we will focus on what you can do with what you have right now. First, we will guide you in assessing your capacity to perform EA in an acquisition. Second, we will focus on the process of engagement: how you start and how you move from an initial foothold. Finally, in the last chapter we summarize the key lessons learned and give some personal advice reflecting on our experiences from taking part in journeys towards EA engagement in acquisitions.

Chapter 8
Your Capacity to Perform

The kind of sophisticated EA capability that some of the multinational serial acquirers possess are rare to see. Some of these companies have been actively developing their EA capabilities for a long time, and with more than 200 acquisitions in the past decades, have had ample opportunities to practice EA in the context of acquiring various companies. Most likely, you and your EA organization are not as fully developed as these companies. And even if you are, going for the whole lot—aspiring for full leverage of EA all at once—may not be advisable. You will need to make sure that you are not biting off more than you can chew.

Depending on how advanced your EA capability is, some of the uses for EA are more readily accessible than others. In this chapter, we match four different levels of EA maturity with the different EA activities in an acquisition process, in order to demonstrate that while not all organizations can reap the full potential of EA at once, all can do something to get the journey going.

Understanding Your EA Maturity

Even if your EA organization is taking its first baby steps—wrestling to get a grip on what digital components actually exist in your landscape and what their purposes are—you can still perform a limited set of EA activities during an acquisition process. On the other hand, for organizations that have EA capabilities that are somewhere in between a very traditional technical documentation and a fully advanced EA capability, there are more opportunities for engagement. Understanding where you are, aka your EA maturity, is the fundament to devising activities within your reach.

There is no shortage of models and frameworks on the market that suggest how to grasp the maturity of your EA capability (Meyer et al. 2011). Models are simplifications that highlight certain aspects of particular importance when considering a specific objective. Because we want to get a grip on how a particular EA capability stands relative to the idealized advanced EA capability, we measure maturity relative

© Springer Nature Switzerland AG 2020   87
S. Henningsson, G. N. Toppenberg, *Architecting Growth in the Digital Era*,
https://doi.org/10.1007/978-3-030-39482-0_8

to the two defining qualities of an advanced EA capability: the *holistic* quality and the *engagement* quality.

Recall from Chap. 3 that the holistic quality refers to EA breaking out from the traditional focus on technical components: IT infrastructures and applications. A holistic quality means that EA is also mandated and able to cover the operational and strategic layers of the organizational domain in its architecting. EA contributes to the defining of organizational capabilities and in formulating strategic aspirations.

The engagement quality refers to a situation where EA is actively participating in organizational transformations. The focus is on architecting as an activity. Instead of passing on blueprints and capability maps to decision-makers, EA is engaged to perform activities such as scenario development, gaps assessment, and roadmap development because of its unique ability to do this through activities of architecting.

You can use the Assessment framework in Box 8.1 to analyze your current EA maturity along these two dimensions. Then, using your scoring we suggest that you reflect on how you position your company's EA capability along the holistic and engaged dimensions.

Box 8.1 Enterprise Architecture Maturity Self-Assessment To get started in your journey to leverage EA for acquisition-based growth, you first need to understand your starting point. Do you have an Advanced EA capability already? Or is your EA capability better characterized as Traditional, Active, or Aspirational? We have created a simple quiz to help you understand your EA maturity based on the qualities required for engaging EA in acquisitions.

First, think about how your EA function is working with EA artifacts, such as references models, capability maps, heat maps, roadmaps, etc. Then, think about what these maps primarily describe; technical fundaments, systems landscapes, organizational capabilities, or strategic aspirations. Now, having these models in mind, rate how your EA capability fits with the statements below about a holistic quality.

Use a scale from 1 to 7, where 1 = strongly disagree; 4 = neutral; and 7 = strongly agree.

1. *EA Models and Documentation:*
   Our EA team manage and maintain capabilities roadmaps and heat maps.
2. *EAs Role in Strategic Planning:*
   Our business and IT planning enables efficiency, agility in extended enterprise.
3. *Architecture Planning:*
   Our planning includes extended enterprise capabilities and adapts to iteration.
4. *Enterprise Architecture Framework*:
   Our EA framework is capability based and focused on planning.
5. *Enterprise Architecture Documents*:
   EA documents are used by decision-makers for business decisions.

(continued)

Box 8.1 (continued)

Your total score is your holistic EA score!

Next, think about the role your EA team is playing in the transformation where it is engaged today. Recall the people initiating the tasks and whether EA is an order-taking organization that executes on whatever is given to it, or if it reaches out and makes suggestions. Reflect on a typical meeting where key decisions are made, and if architects are seen as equal members of the team when developing plans for how to evolve the organization. Now, having these reflections in mind, rate how your EA capability fits with the statements below about your engaged quality.

Use a scale from 1 to 7, where 1 = strongly disagree; 4 = neutral; and 7 = strongly agree.

6. *Response to Change*:
   Our business and IT governance continuously improves to respond to change.
7. *Measuring EAs value*:
   We measure business and IT performance metrics to show connections.
8. *Communication and Influence*:
   We proactively communicate and seek feedback with business stakeholders.
9. *Enterprise Change*:
   Our EA team and outputs are used in enterprise planning.
10. *The company perception of EA*:
    EA is perceived as having a positive and direct impact on enterprise change.

Your total score is your engaged EA score!

Now, use the scores of your holistic and engaged EA quality in the EA capability maturity matrix of Fig. 8.1. Doing so will give you a basic idea of the starting point for your journey. Scores for the holistic quality range from 10 to 70. A score from 10 to 40 indicates you are in the left-hand side of the figure, while a score from 41 to 70 puts you in the right-hand side of the matrix.

Scores for the engaged quality also range from 10 to 70. A score from 10 to 40 indicates that you are in the bottom half of the figure, while a score from 41 to 70 puts you in the top half.

You can do this as a self-assessment and compare it with the results that your colleagues get it when they make the assessment, or make it a group exercise and go through the questions together while discussing and agreeing on the score. In the end, try to agree upon where in the matrix you are placing yourself. While this is a subjective measurement that is likely to be biased on recent victories or shortcomings, it forms a baseline for more in-depth discussions on what to do next. Then, when you are ready, use the advice in Part II to start your journey!

Positioned along the holistic and engaged quality dimensions, we identify four different levels of EA capability: Traditional, Active, Aspirational, and Advanced (Fig. 8.1). The most basic level is the Traditional EA capability that is confined to a technical documentation purpose. The Active and Aspirational EA capabilities both represent higher degrees of maturity, with enhancements in both the engaged and holistic qualities, respectively. The fully Advanced EA capability presents both these qualities. In the remainder of this chapter, we investigate in detail what capacity to perform these different levels of maturity warrants relative to the acquisition process.

Traditional EA: Documenting the Technical Transformation

The most basic EA capability maturity is the *Traditional EA capability*. This is an EA capability that is passive in the sense that it creates EA artifacts in reaction to what others order from it. These artifacts span the technical layers of the organization. Typically, the Head of EA would in this organization report to the CTO or another technical lead. The mentality of the architects is an order-taking mentality, with no advisory mandate. Tasks in which EA is activated would be in relation to

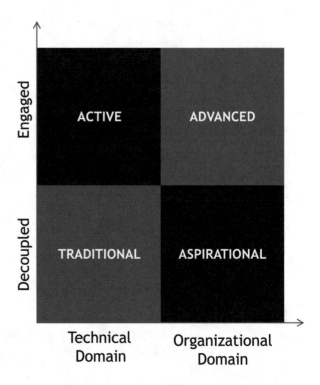

Fig. 8.1 EA maturity model based on engagement quality and holistic quality (©2019 The Authors, reprinted with permission)

cost savings and rationalizations, where the output of EA is used by decision-makers as one of several starting points to form decisions on where to cut the budget.

The mandate of the Traditional EA capability is to provide technical documentation. You can see how this capability can be used in a limited set of activities in the acquisition process (Table 8.1). Let us examine the role of Traditional EA capability in these phases. One thing even the most basic EA capability can do is to provide documentation of the acquirer's own IT landscape as the starting point. As we discussed earlier in the book, understanding the acquirer's own setup is one of the key activities in the acquisition preparation phase, which positions the acquirer to move rapidly once a specific acquisition target has been identified. Because the Traditional EA capability only works with the technical layers of the organization, it limits documentation.

During the selection phase, in reference to the identification and assessment of potential integration targets, the Traditional EA capability would have limited possibilities to contribute. It has been suggested that because technological fit between acquirer and target makes integration easier, technical documentation should also guide the selection process. It is, however, unrealistic that this would be the case for a traditional company where IT has a supporting role. For a company with a significant digital offering, such as a software company, it would be critical to document the fit between offerings, but this would not be a task assigned to a Traditional EA capability.

On the other hand, in the integration phase, a Traditional EA capability can contribute significantly to the roadmap development. From the perspective of a Traditional EA capability, acquisitions are oddities that need to be dealt with. They create overlapping and redundant IT capabilities that can be rationalized for increased efficiency. Developing, or at least documenting, the roadmap to the new target state is a suitable task for a traditional EA capability.

Along the same lines, EA can contribute to integration evaluation by measuring the extent that the acquisition project has introduced technical inconsistencies that are likely to impede the organization in the future. As EA has been engaged in documenting the as-is state, the technical roadmap towards an envisioned to-be scenario, these can be contrasted with the actual developments and contribute to the final to-be scenario. Therefore, even without engaging EA in the actual evaluation of the acquisition these basic artifacts provide evaluators with technical traceability.

Active EA: Defining the Technical Transformation

An EA capability that has matured from passive to engaged but still only works within the technical layers of the organization is an *Active EA capability*. Here, EA is not only taking orders, but actively contributing to the strategic formulations, albeit still only on a technical level. Architects can reach out and engage in organizational transformation to ensure an end-to-end coherence of the IT landscape. In this maturity level, the Head of EA would typically report to the CIO and be activated to determine the target state of the IT landscape in organizational transformations.

Table 8.1 Levels of EA maturity and capacities to impact the acquisition process

EA capability maturity		Acquisition process				
		Preparation	Selection	Integration	Continuation
	Traditional	Documentation (technical)		Roadmap development (technical)	Integration evaluation (technical)
	Active	Infrastructure preparation Platformization	Suite analysis Roadblock analysis Platform consistency modelling	IT enablement Carve-out bridging	
	Aspirational	Documentation (organizational)	Transformation needs assessment Identification of nontransferable enablers	Roadmap development (organizational)	Integration evaluation (organizational)
	Advanced	Knowledge integration Gap exposure	Business case estimation Discovery of reverse integration potential	To be state definition Organizational design	Integration correction

The Active EA capability is able to accomplish all the tasks that were attributed to the traditional EA capability above, and some more that resonate with its capacity to drive the technical side of transformations. Similar to how we examined Traditional EA, we will go through these phases one by one. In the preparation phase, a suitable task for an Active EA capability is the infrastructure preparation. This task concerns investigating and updating the IT infrastructure so that it can be modified to meet a specified range of possible acquisition scenarios, for example, to ensure that key systems can handle data volume increases following an acquisition. A version of infrastructure preparation is platformization, in which a corporate core layer is decoupled from a business-unit-specific layer. This requires that EA be able to actively drive enabling projects, but as most of the work is technical enablement, it is a task suitable for an Active EA capability.

In the selection phase, the Active EA capability can play an important role despite not working with the organizational layers of the organization. This is particularly true if the acquisition has a substantial digital footprint, meaning that the digital products and services provided by the acquisition target forms part of the value calculations driving the acquisition. Given the in-depth understanding of how technologies combine in the acquirer's existing landscape, the Active EA capability can be engaged to perform the suite analysis of how digital offerings fit technologically. The technical roadblock analysis is also a matching activity for an Active EA capability, as this requires inspection of how an integration scenario would actually play out on a technical level. Furthermore, a platform consistency mapping requires the active contribution of EA to actually inspect how the potential acquisition is technologically enabled and how the acquirer's platform matches this enablement.

An Active EA capability means that EA is the corporate expert function for how business capabilities are enabled by technical capabilities. Therefore, charging the Active EA capability with the task of forming the IT enablement scenario of the combined organizations is natural. Instead of passing on documentation of the as-is state to a specific IT integration function, EA at this maturity is fit for active participation in making the technical to-be scenario. In the carve-out bridging analysis, an Active EA capability will be engaged to assess the shortest route (maximal reuse) route to cover a gap in the technological provisioning between acquirer and vendor of a divestment acquisition. This will also give EA insights into why certain decisions are made, which at a later stage can inform the general development roadmaps for the company.

Aspirational EA: Informing the Organizational Transformation

An Aspirational EA capability is an EA capability that has matured beyond technical documentation to cover also the operational capabilities of the organization. That is, documentation now also includes which operational capabilities are enabled by which technical capabilities, and how operational capabilities should transform to reach target states. Ideally, the Head of EA would report to the COO to channel the output adequately and the EA team needs to comprise also business architects that design the state and evolution of operational capabilities. Beyond cost cutting and rationalization on the technical side of the organization, the Aspirational EA capability is active in relation to organizational optimizations.

The Aspirational EA capability is able to accomplish all the tasks that were attributed to the Traditional EA capability. Compared to the Active EA capability, the Aspirational capability is still based on a passive, order-taking mentality, but has on the other hand matured to include also the organizational layers in its documenting function. This gives the possibility to document and inform not only the technical integration, but also the organizational integration in the acquisition. Specifically, in the preparation phase, the Aspirational EA capability is suited to document the as-is state of the acquirer both at the technical and organizational level.

Because it spans out into the organizational layers of the company, the Aspirational EA capability can also contribute to the transformation needs assessment. Note, at this maturity the EA capability would not be fit for, or allowed to, actually collaborate on the task. What Aspirational EA is capable of is to provide the foundational material for assessing transformation need, including capability heat maps depicting both the organizational and technical transformation needs. This will speed up the up the assessment process since it enables communication of key transformational areas and documents intentions for later evaluation. This includes documenting the nontransferable enablers of a divested business in the specific case of a divestment acquisition. Because EA is operating in a passive mode, EA would, when asked, document these and notify decision-makers, but would not be in charge of resolving the complication of identified nontransferable enablers.

If EA has been contributing to the documentation of the as-is scenario, the to-be scenario, and the transformation needs, then EA is also well positioned to contribute to the evaluation of the acquisition. In the same way that the Traditional EA capability can give transparence to the technical integration project, an Aspirational EA capability can furthermore provide similar transparency to the organizational integration project. This would include contributing to integration evaluation by measuring the extent that the acquisition project has introduced organizational inconsistencies that muddle decision responsibility and makes it difficult for the organization to evolve as a coherent whole.

Advanced EA: Orchestrating the Organizational Transformation

The fully Advanced EA capability portrays both the engagement quality and holistic quality. As such it is active in orchestrating organizational transformations across all layers of the organization. To be effective, an EA capability at this maturity would report to, or have otherwise close connections to, the organization's key transformation managers, including the CFO and business development managers overseeing activities such as market entries, R&D, alliances, and acquisitions.

The Advanced EA capability is fit to actively perform all tasks described in Chaps. 4–7. Compared to the less mature EA capabilities, what sets the Advanced EA capability apart is that it is fit to actively participate in the unfolding of the acquisition process, by assuming responsibility for subtasks relating to the orchestration of the business and technological capability landscapes.

The Advanced EA capability is organized in cross-functional teams that actively take part in orchestrating organizational transformation. A capability at this level of maturity is therefore fit to deliver on knowledge integration across organizational levels, building a holistic understanding of how the organizational layers fit together. Because the Advanced EA capability is a trusted partner in organizational transformations, the EA team can also be entrusted to indicate gaps in the capability landscapes that can feed into the search for suitable acquisition targets to address these gaps.

In the selection phase, the business case motivating the acquisition is a forward projection of how the organizations will combine, and the synergies that can be derived from this combination. The Advanced EA capability is fit to participate in this work by modelling the acquisition target, and through overlaying it with the acquirer's existing capability maps, identifying possibilities for cost rationalization as well as combinatory enhancement. This activity can be bidirectional, meaning that Advanced EA can examine the target for specific capabilities that are worth preserving and reverse integrating into the acquirer, so as not to miss possible business benefits in the integration.

In the integration phase, the Advance EA capability is fit to contribute both to the technical to-be state definition and the organizational design. When during the integration phase additional discoveries are made about the target, both at the organizational and technical levels, EA can rapidly assess the impact of these discoveries and how they implicate across the organizational layers. To be able to do this, EA must be actively engage in the process when these discoveries are made. Therefore, this use of EA is likely only to be effective for Advanced EA capabilities, and not less mature EA capabilities.

Lastly, because the Advanced EA capability is an active driver of organizational transformation, EA is naturally suited for picking up the transformation from where the acquisition projects left off. Typically, this will be a suboptimal state that delivers on the key acquisition benefits, but with introduced complexity and ideal integration solutions that have been pushed to become general business improvement activities. In order to not leave these issues unattended after the acquisition project is dissolved, handing over the task to EA to drive long-term corrective activities, both in the business and technical layers of the combined organization, is appropriate when an Advanced EA capability is present. Doing so requires EA to have a holistic, orchestrating role in the ongoing transformation of the organization where issues rooted in the acquisition are considered in relation to other transformational initiatives. The Advanced EA capability is in this way tasked to orchestrate the continuation phase of one acquisition project transition into the preparation of the next acquisition.

Chapter Key Points

- Depending on how advanced your EA capability is, some of the EA uses are more readily accessible than others.
- Understanding where you are, your EA maturity, is the fundament to devising activities within its reach.
- In the context of acquisitions, EA capability maturity can be defined with basis in the two qualities of an advanced EA capability: the *holistic* quality and the *engagement* quality.
- The *Traditional EA capability* has a technical documentation mandate. This capability can support the acquisition process through executing orders on documenting the technical landscapes at different points in the process.
- The *Active EA capability* has a mandate to engage in the technical development trajectory of the company. In the acquisition process, this capability can collaborate to drive the technical enablement of the acquisition.
- The *Aspirational EA capability* has a documentation mandate that reaches into the business levels of the organization. This capability can be used to document and inform not only the technical integration, but also the organizational integration in the acquisition.
- The *Advanced EA capability* has a mandate to engage in delivering knowledge integration across organizational levels. This capability can be used to effectively orchestrate the acquisition and its relations to other of organizational transformations.

Reference

Meyer, M., Helfert, M., & O'Brien, C. (2011, October). An analysis of enterprise architecture maturity frameworks. In: J. Grabis & M. Kirikova (Eds.), *International Conference on Business Informatics Research (BIR 2011)* (pp. 167–177), Riga, Latvia. Heidelberg: Springer.

Chapter 9
Getting Your Foot in the Door and Beyond

Now it is your turn to get going! So, you are an EA leader and you have an EA capability with some level of maturity, but your organization is not leveraging EA in acquisitions. Or, you may be responsible for a part of the acquisition integration in a company that is not leveraging EA in the acquisition process. All organizations with an EA capability can contribute to an acquisition project, no matter how nascent that capability is. This means that your organization has a developed tool in the corporate toolbox that is sitting idle and not being put to use. This is a waste of resources and it is your task to change that.

In this chapter we focus on where the journey of activating EA in acquisition starts, and how you can proceed from an initial foothold. First, we start with the initial activities to address how to formulate the argument for activating EA and whom to address your EA pitch. Then we turn to the process of increasing the footprint. This requires understanding the current match between capacity and mandate of EA—how to achieve a sound balance between activities that build the EA capability and activities that put it to work.

Entry: Get Started

All journeys start somewhere and with something, but where and how? It is very unlikely that an EA leader can successfully argue that because EA is really advanced it should be part of driving the acquisition. There are good causes for this. Just as EA is a particular knowledge domain that an acquisition expert cannot be expected to master, acquisitions represent a particular knowledge domain that an EA leader cannot be expected to master right from the start. Acquisitions have a very particular dynamic in the stages leading up to deal closure, which is greatly impacted by legal constraints, and follows evolutionary life cycles not seen elsewhere that are deeply embedded into social and political structures. With high values at stake, it takes very little error to cause extensive damage. Therefore, an organization with an acquisition

© Springer Nature Switzerland AG 2020
S. Henningsson, G. N. Toppenberg, *Architecting Growth in the Digital Era*,
https://doi.org/10.1007/978-3-030-39482-0_9

Fig. 9.1 Arguing the case for EA in acquisitions

protocol that somewhat works, despite minor glitches, is typically reluctant to explore new ways that radically depart from the existing way of doing things. The risk is too high.

It follows that all journeys towards leveraging EA in acquisitions start small, with the most basic activities that provide opportunities to, but not commitment from, the people involved in managing and making acquisitions. These basic activities are to be found in the bottom left corner of the maturity model, associated with the traditional EA capability. The ambition is to hand over artifacts to the acquisition makers that will help them accomplish their tasks in an improved way.

To get started, it is critical to define an entry strategy based on the pain points you are suggesting to solve, the owner of those pain points, and the value that EA brings relative to the pain points (Fig. 9.1).

In most cases, the very first influence that EA has on acquisitions is through the technical capability maps of the acquirer. The audience most receptive to thinking in terms of capabilities tend to be working with the IT integration. For IT employees, architecture is well established as a part of the IT organization's practice and they understand what forms the baseline to which the acquisition should be integrated. Therefore, with the blueprint of the acquirer's IT landscape, the IT integration team can travel to the potential target and examine what target equivalents look like, make assumptions where no information is available, and put question marks where IT components appear to have no match at the acquirer.

The second activity that follows naturally from the use of capability maps as input for examining the target is the articulation of the to-be scenario as capability maps, and IT development as capability roadmaps. For this to be the case, it is likely that the acquisition managers responsible for IT integration have seen the value of capability maps in the target examination and have become familiar with this way of expressing scenarios. Exposure should have presented the advantages of thinking in capabilities. When this is the case, EA can take orders from the acquisition managers to develop to-be scenarios and roadmaps for communication and documentation purposes. Likely, this is at first going to take place in parallel to the usual way the company describes the future state of the merged organization, because of the high risk of changing practices.

Because these basic activities are where it makes sense to start the journey towards involving EA in acquisitions, from a communication perspective the starting point for arguing the need for acquisition falls on the individual, typically a senior manager, that is responsible for the IT integration in acquisition. For instance, this would be the managers that own the problem that EA initially would solve.

To start the conversation about involving EA in acquisitions, it is critical to first do a bit of homework, analyzing past acquisitions, or, if the company has not undertaken any acquisitions yet, well-known acquisitions by competitors. This analysis should focus on specific points with improvement potential in these acquisitions. Such improvements could be related to time, cost, synergistic potential, or long-term effects—that is, pain points.

Particularly compelling cases that link well to the potential of EA are acquisitions where expensive surprises were identified at a late stage in the acquisition process and cases where the integration processes were sluggish, and where the blame was cast on IT. These "pain points" are very concrete and directly owned by the manager being addressed in the pitch. Relevant issues pertaining to the induced complexity of the infrastructure are simply more abstract and harder to measure. Complexity does not hurt right now, it hurts in the future. In addition, the owner of the issue is likely a general IT manager and not the same manager that is in charge of IT in acquisition.

By using the past, or otherwise known issues, as the basis of your presentation, it is then possible to outline EA capabilities in acquisition around three simple value principles:

- *Faster time to synergy.* EA can, through pre-acquisition documentation, enable acquisition selection and integration work to hit the ground running, catalyze planning, and make the acquisition reach a state of benefit realization fast.
- *Fewer (expensive) surprises.* Through involvement of EA, it becomes more transparent what are the risk areas and where costly problems may arise.
- *No mess that isn't worth it.* While it might be necessary to depart from ideal integration solutions and to make quick fixes to hit deadlines, EA can help make such actions considerate decisions and to document the integration debt the actions cause.

A simple presentation with identified pain points of the past, illustrations on how the challenges would have been met if EA had been involved, and a presentation slide with the three bullet points above is a powerful argumentation for why they should start the journey. This presentation does not address the full potential of EA and all the different ways that a fully advanced EA capability could leverage of course. Instead it is focused on the immediate value of the initial activities for the problem holder. This is to create a first foothold in the acquisition process that then can be expanded.

Increasing Engagement: Capacity and Mandate

Once a foothold has been established, it is possible to increase the involvement of EA in acquisitions through a vicarious circle of positive impact, which triggers additional involvement. This vicarious circle combines three different development processes (Fig. 9.2). The first is the process by which EA's mandate to perform is developing towards its capacity to perform. The second is the process by which EA is learning about the acquisition context, including the particularities of working in an acquisition project. The third is the process of building the EA capability, increasing its capacity to perform.

The vicarious circle is thus based on the fact that EA always is able to deliver on the tasks it takes on. Therefore, any progression is dependent on an appropriate understanding of EA's capacity relative to its mandate to perform. The capacity to perform is reflected in the maturity of EA (see Fig. 8.1). For an EA capacity with either Active, Aspirational, or Advanced maturity, there is possibility to reach beyond the initial foothold. However, an Active or Aspirational EA capability holds different unused capacity, which sets the frame for how to develop from the initial foothold.

For an Active EA capability, the development step is to become an active collaborator in the acquisition process, taking on tasks that include infrastructure preparation, suite and roadblock analysis, and determining the ideal IT enablement of the combined organization. These are activities that stay within the IT domain of

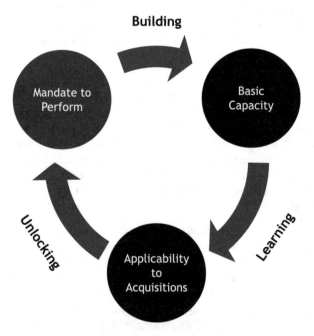

Fig. 9.2 The vicarious circle of increasing EA engagement in acquisitions

the acquisition. This means that EA will interact with the same acquisition manager responsible for IT integration. Clearly, the most convincing argument is based on past success. It is unlikely that any EA leader can argue an active role of EA in acquisitions before there is a track record of past successes, since standard acquisition protocols do not include the use of EA.

For an Aspirational EA capability, the development step beyond the basic use of documenting IT states is to also perform a similar documenting function for the business side of the acquisition. In one way, this is an easier sell than active engagement because it does not require convincing any acquisition manager to reallocate task responsibility. Documentation of the business side, the strategic and operational levels of the target, through EA can take place in parallel with ordinary acquisition activities. However, what makes progression in this direction difficult is that the EA team has to approach a new manager, one that is more generally responsible for the acquisition beyond the IT issues. The arguments and value propositions would be similar to when establishing the initial foothold, but the target audience is likely to be less familiar with thinking in terms of capability maps. EA does not have the same history of working with the business layers of organizations.

For companies with fully Advanced EA capabilities, the possible progression paths from basic involvement includes both trajectories described above. For the EA leader, the task is to determine which conversation is the most feasible: to convince the acquisition IT lead to increase the involvement of EA to an active collaborator, or to convince the general acquisition manager to try out capability thinking. A hint to answering this question can be found in where the most important successes have been in the past. If there are clear wins on the IT side of the acquisition, moving to active involvement would be a feasible conversation. If there are clear wins of capability thinking on the business side of other types of organizational transformations, the latter conversation should be feasible. If there are no substantial successes to draw on at all? Then it is probably not time yet to increase the involvement. Instead, focus on the second or third development processes.

The second development process, the one of learning the context-specific dynamics of acquisitions, fits the argument of starting small and only progressing when initial success is established. For the acquisition IT manager to allocate subtasks to EA, it is critical that EA can work in this context. The knowledge about acquisition is highly tacit and can to some extent only be learnt by taking part in these processes and reflecting on outcomes. Reflection should be done in a formalized way, where actions and their outcomes are discussed among members of the acquisition project. This is because acquisitions are highly ambiguous: it is difficult both to judge the overall outcome (positive or negative) and particularly difficult to determine what led to a specific outcome. Was the outcome successful despite or because of the involvement of EA? Was the delay a consequence of spending time on capability maps, or would a different approach to analysis have led to an even longer delay? Answers to questions like these will never be certain, but through conversations with participants in the acquisition, an understanding of the role EA played can be better understood.

In addition, undertaking serious evaluations of EA also serves a communication purpose. Getting a basic involvement is an important step for EA. From a communication perspective, evaluation of the contribution of EA channels attention to what it meant not only within the EA team, but more importantly, also generally in the acquisition project. EA cannot build further on past successes, unless everyone is aware of the successes. In addition, evaluating the role of EA also signals that the EA team is prepared to listen and take feedback into consideration in order to improve. This is an important signal to the acquisition team.

The third development process contributing to the involvement of EA in acquisitions is the general progression of the EA maturity. The overall capacity of EA puts a limitation on the extent of involvement. If the EA capability has the maturity of a Traditional EA capability, success cannot lead to increased involvement without capability building.

The general task of EA capability building falls outside the scope of this book. However, with specific reference to the involvement in acquisitions, it is important to recognize that activities beyond learning by doing are required. Employing a Traditional EA capability to perform basic activities in acquisitions makes the EA team better and better in performing these roles, but teaches the team very little on how to become an Active EA capability. For this, the team needs to go beyond activity repetition to explore new ways of working.

This creates a dilemma, a tension between using the EA capacity at a given performance level or investing in it to create a greater capacity to benefit from subsequently. On a practical level, should members of the EA team on a given day *architect* or *learn how to architect*? To make the relationship between these two activities even more complex, architecting demonstrates the value of EA, which in turn can give more resources for learning at a later stage. Only focusing on learning and not putting built capacity to use will soon raise the question what value EA actually brings to the table. Therefore, finding the right balance between *usage* and *building* in EA is a key dilemma that is relevant way beyond the acquisition context, but is a balance that is particularly relevant here as it is clearly so that increased capability clearly allows for increased involvement.

Chapter Key Points

- Acquisitions are particular organizational transformations with distinct dynamics, deadlines, politics, and priorities compared to other transformations that anyone involved needs to master.
- The value that EA delivers in acquisitions can be communicated based on three simple value principles: *faster time to synergy, fewer surprises,* and *no mess that isn't worth it.*
- The journey of putting EA into acquisitions starts small with the establishment of a fundamental foothold in the basic uses of EA, no matter the how advanced the EA capability is.

- An appropriate starting point is the provision of as-is capability maps of the acquirer and the documentation of the intended to-be state following the integration.
- Increasing the engagement follows an analysis of EA's capacity to perform in relation to the mandate given.
- Increased involvement of EA in acquisitions is achieved through a vicarious circle of positive impacts which triggers additional involvement.
- To expand the capacity of EA, it is necessary to break free from incremental refinement and find a good balance between actual architecting and learning how to architect.

Chapter 10
A Note for the Journey

We have written this book to give you the cognitive tools and practical guidelines to leverage EA in order to enable value-creating corporate acquisitions. Our research and practical work with dozens of acquisitions shows that EA can play a major role in these critical, complex events. Hopefully, we have given you plenty of examples in this book as evidence to illustrate the need for bringing EA into the acquisition process.

In this last chapter of the book, we will take on a more personal tone and present some of our reflections on the use of EA in acquisition. Having studied and worked with both EA and acquisitions for more than a decade now, we have seen patterns in the past that in their extension bear witness of future developments. Most importantly, the need for EA in acquisitions is growing with every new piece of the technology that is introduced into business. This means that the challenges EA has to address are accentuated, but so are the rewards if it is effectively used.

Acquisitions Can Mean a Breakthrough for Enterprise Architecture

Is there anything more frustrating than being an EA manager that simply does not get the chance to contribute to solving important problems? Well, if so, it could be having to work with EA managers that cannot accept that the purpose of the company is not to have a nice architecture, but to do great business.

In one company, we talked with an EA manager that was hired to revamp the EA practice for a digital age, taking an end-to-end responsibility for how the company used digital technologies. But what happened was that he had no actual decision power. In the end, he felt that the company ignored his advice. He described the feeling as sitting in a bus going at maximum speed on the highway, and being the

© Springer Nature Switzerland AG 2020
S. Henningsson, G. N. Toppenberg, *Architecting Growth in the Digital Era*,
https://doi.org/10.1007/978-3-030-39482-0_10

only one who was concerned that the whole thing was falling apart. Everyone else was just screaming "Faster, faster!"

We also talked with a business manager who openly confessed that they tried to schedule planning meetings when the architects were travelling, were offsite with the teams, or for other reasons were not able to "damage the business." And, we spoke with one senior director of acquisitions who said she would never allow EA into the acquisition process, because then the whole acquisition discussion would be about problems with systems compatibility and not about how to develop the business.

We had much difficulties in picking one of the two as the most frustrating. We have seen both occurring many times, and both could be pretty ugly when played out in the acquisition context. We have seen anger and resentment. But, we have also seen a lot of passion and potential!

For EA architects and managers, acquisitions are opportunities to showcase what EA can do for the company. In our view, there is no time that an advanced EA capability is more useful or more visible than during an acquisition. It is in these situations, where firms struggle with complex organizational transformations that cut across all layers, under severe time pressure to conclude the consolidation, with massive values at stake, that EA can shine. *Because this is difficult*, it is a perfect job for EA. EA is a discipline that has been formed to deal with complexity and dependencies while not losing track of the bigger picture and what really matters to the firm.

If EA can get a foothold into the acquisition game and subsequently build the mandate to play, that can be the breakthrough for EA as a recognized enabler of corporate strategy. Acquisitions are challenging tasks with few, if any, equals in the corporate world. With high rewards enticing the pursuit, but with massive risks looming in the background, acquisitions typically capture the full attention of the acquirer. Acquisitions also form very good stories, with dramatic plots that include heroes, villains, and even casualties. This makes the media very keen to report on any move taken. Therefore, acquisitions are where careers are made, or broken.

If effectively leveraged in acquisitions, the firm gets a showcase for the potential of EA. In the process, EA earns a set of internal advocates that see the value and are used to working with the EA practices. Even more importantly, the company gains a set of individuals that are ready to entrust EA with some of the most critical tasks of important strategic transformations. The acquisition situation can spur capacity investment, foster learning experiences, and earn EA recognition that can catalyze EA work way beyond the acquisition context. Therefore, getting EA into the acquisition process could be the breakthrough that many EA leaders are desperately craving.

EA Is About Having Fewer Problems and Better Solutions

When we interviewed the CFO of the global food ingredients company Danisco about his acquisition experiences, he said that they had a very strange CIO in Danisco. In all the previous places where the CFO had worked, the CIOs had reacted with a terrified face to all news about acquiring. They all knew that acquisition were high-stake games in which IT would always be asked to work out a solution for the combined business organization that was already signed off on. The chances of IT messing things up were statistically about 50%, so understandably the CIOs were walking home at night with a growing headache.

In Danisco, the CIO used to clap his hands with excitement when there was an acquisition announced. Because this was his moment to shine. All the hard work of setting up the business and technical layers to enable growth would eventually pay off. The acquisition team that Danisco could put on the deal-making and integration job had deep technical knowledge and understood how all layers fitted together. In fact, the CIO himself was in many cases leading the operational due diligence and the overall integration project. Why Danisco was a very successful acquirer was because they had set themselves up to have few problems in the acquisition, they set up the deals to generate few new problems and they had the right people in place to deal with the few problems that emerged.

There is no doubt that acquisitions could be done without EA. To the same extent that the history is replete with example of failed acquisitions, it is also full of example of successful acquisitions. We are not saying that you cannot do acquisitions well without EA, *but why would you?* You can do well by finding other ways to solve problems, by having extremely clever people working on the task or by being lucky. But if you do not want to be dependent on luck, we say: consider EA! EA is a powerful tool to achieve exactly what Danisco achieved. You can have coherent business and technology layers that support growth without EA, but your chances of succeeding with it dramatically increases when you draw on EA. You can craft integration solutions that balance short-term benefits with long-term consistency and performance considerations, but we promise you that the chances of this skyrocket if you use a systemic approach to it rather than rely on ad hoc problem solving. Why depend on luck, when you do not have to?

Principles for Introducing EA in Acquisitions

While every firm is unique and the prospect of EA is different in every acquisition, yet having worked with dozens of firms embarking on this journey, there are some practices that stand out as more effective than others. In our experience, successful introduction of EA in the acquisition process tends to follow four broad principles: *recognize limitations, start where you are, learn on the job,* and *continuously work on your sales pitch.*

First, understand what EA is suited to do and what falls outside the scope of EA practice. Acquisitions are complex organizational transformations, with a range of problems for which EA is not the solution. Do not try to involve EA in issues of change management, cultural clashes, people management, or other similar important aspects of the acquisition for which it is not suited. Remember, a kid with a new hammer sees nails everywhere. It is important to stay true to what problems EA actually solves and in addition recognize that there are particular dynamics of the acquisition that an EA leader without acquisition experience will not fully understand at the beginning. Therefore, at least for a start, focus on the jobs that EA knows how to do and are likely to give initial success.

Second, start with what you have, not with what you would like to have as EA capability in the future. Capability building takes time and requires extensive organizational support. If you are a traditional EA department, this is what you have to work with. By the time you have figured out how to use the potential of the traditional EA capability, things might have changed. The value of EA could be more generally accepted, and new technology strategies or moves by rival firms may have paved the ground for boosting EA. If not, you might need to focus more explicitly on building your capacity to match a growing mandate to play, so for now, getting going and producing real value is your first priority.

Third, learn. Learning within the acquisition context is surprisingly difficult. In fact, much research points to the fact that very few acquirers learn anything useful from one acquisition to the next. It is hard to place value on the multifaceted outcomes of acquisitions and the complex nets of causality that interact to form outcomes. So, do not expect that doing will automatically translate into learning. Instead, formal and dedicated evaluation is critical for learning. But do not put too much emphasis on evaluation reports. See the evaluation *process* as important in enabling people to connect the dots and to understand the links between actions and outcomes. Use the same individuals across the process to follow acquisitions from initial idea to integration completion. Make EA take a lead in evaluation.

Fourth, have a sales pitch ready to explain the value that EA brings to acquisitions. Be specific and contextualize with past experiences: where could EA have led to problems being avoided or surfaced additional opportunities. Importantly, remember that the value of EA changes over time. The arguments for leveraging traditional usage of EA in technical documentation are not the same as for extending the role of EA from passive to active use in the process. Therefore, continuously work on the sales pitch for the next step you want EA to take.

Following these four principles will not solve all problems or earn EA a place at the acquisition table by itself. Yet, in our experience, it is surprisingly often that these four simple processes have been part of the retrospective story explaining an acquisition's success. Focusing attention on these basic pillars of scoping, learning, and arguing for EA is a very good start to get going.

Grow with the Digital Challenge

We started this book with the continuous permeation of digital technology in business being the fundamental premise for why you should turn to EA as an enabler of value-creating acquisitions. From gaining a critical supporting role for operations, digital technologies are now becoming inseparable from business operations. Almost all physical products and services are being infused or connected with digital elements. We drive cars with sensors in them, chat with our doctors over video, book upcoming trips by interacting with virtual sales agents, entrust our savings to trading algorithms, and have mobile phone apps to keep track of our medicines.

Digital is also permeating back-office functions and internal processes. Manufacturing robots used to be extremely expensive and reserved only for very high-demanding tasks. Now they are becoming advanced commodities, with extended use for a fraction of the cost. We can 3D-print spare parts for engineered equipment and use augmented reality for remote surgery. Artificial intelligence is taking over route planning in logistics, scheduling in production, and quality assurance in chemical process industries.

In the intersection between the internal and external of firms, products and services are sold over digital marketplaces and through online auctions. When we need more complex interactions, we are greeted by virtual assistants for booking hairdressers, dinner reservations, and travels. Even personalized customer service is boosted by natural language processing and machine learning to reduce cost and to deliver superior customer experiences.

With everything being digital and everything being connected, there is an explosion in data. This is an important development because data is the fundament for improvement. Understanding what causes what, why, and under what circumstances is the key enabler of effective change. In the years to come, companies will be using data to become better, smarter, and more rigorous at many key activities: making predictions and forecasts; hiring and promoting people; deciding on product attributes; optimizing internal processes; marketing and advertising; and customizing products and services. Using data for continuous improvement is becoming the new normal, a foundational condition for any kind of business. Firms that do it better will pull ahead of those that struggle to use their opportunities.

While the impact of digitalization this far is massive, leading to mass disruption and changing logics of competition across industry, we can be certain that we have not seen anything yet. Each of the technologies mentioned above are on their own steep development path. This alone will lead to many new uses in the immediate future. But what is even more important to understanding the massive implications ahead is the combinatory nature of digital technology. Digital technologies are much more powerful when used together with other digital technologies. Augmented reality used for educational purpose while training engineers for the risky job of oil rig repairs is fun and effective. But imagine the power of combining augmented reality with repair robots that fly to oil rigs on self-flying drones directed by artificial intelligence to replace components before the break down, as predicted by signals from sensors placed on the rig, which feed data into a maintenance algorithm. The combinatory capacities of digital technologies means that the impact they will have in the future is growing exponentially.

Two things can be said about digitalization and corporate acquisitions. One is that digitalization is putting much more emphasis on technology as an enabler of synergies. Today, synergistic effects in production means on a technological level the integration of two production planning systems. Tomorrow, with extensive use of production robots, those robots need to be considered also in the technological integration scope. Similarly, the merger of two companies that offer physical products fused with digital technologies needs to consider the technological dimension of making these different products possible to be combined and be used together by the customer. Only when connected, digital elements from two previously separated pools will feed data to guide improvements. Digitalization therefore brings the technical integration challenge in acquisitions to a completely new level!

The other important implication of digitalization on acquisitions is the changing nature of acquisition rationales. Beyond the traditional reasons of economies of scale and scope, access to digital technology is in itself becoming an important driver to acquire. This is already true for companies such as Cisco that rely extensively on digital technology acquisitions as a pillar for technological innovation. Now, this practice is growing rapidly. In the automotive industry, for example, we have witnessed a severalfold increase in digital technology acquisitions over the last few years.

Against these digital developments, we can only think that the importance of EA will grow in the future. Today, the job of EA would deal mostly with back-office functions, getting coherence between business capabilities and the technologies that supports them. The technical components discussed will be different forms of enterprise systems supporting production planning, maintenance, supply chains, human resource management, and so on.

In the future, EA would have to move towards the front-end of the company, orchestrating change across digitized products, services, and customer channels. Truly, EA needs to assume end-to-end consistency of all digital technologies used in the company. In an acquisition, digital technology is where the synergies are created, not as a source of enabling business synergies. Therefore, EA needs to embrace also roles related to this expanded permeation of technology. The role of EA in acquisitions will expand.

We've Seen Nothing Yet

Personally, we have thought about EA in relation to acquisitions for more than a decade now. Initially, the match between EA and acquisitions seemed to us a natural fit with high potential on a conceptual level, but we did not see any practical use for it. Eventually, examples started to emerge. We found ourselves more frequently interviewing EA leaders about their involvement as we traced these acquisition processes. Working with EA in practice, we started to see tasks assigned to EA that originated in past acquisitions. Oftentimes, the link was implicit and sometimes the architects working on a task did not even know that they were working with the residual effects of rushed decisions from past acquisitions. Yet, the link was there.

Over time, we started to see more explicit use of EA in acquisitions. And, as the maturity of EA grew we started to see more and more examples of what an advanced EA capability could do. We started to see EA practices that not only threw blueprints over the fence to the deal-making team, but were called on to be part of estimating the synergistic potential or drawing to-be scenarios. What had initially only been a good conceptual idea was evidently also working in practice. With EA gaining the mandate to play, we could learn more about what was practically feasible, critically important, and particularly complex to achieve.

Admittedly, understanding the link between EA and acquisitions is a work in progress. Everywhere we look we find more nuances and more clever uses of EA. EA tools are all continuously becoming more sophisticated and the technologies supporting EA are evolving rapidly. EA today can do so much more than it could 10 years ago, and EA in 5 years will be able to take on a new set of challenges. Understanding the use of EA in acquisitions is the hunt for a running target.

It is our full conviction that even though we have written this book to provide a comprehensive account for the capacity of EA in today's acquisitions, we are sure that we have not seen anything yet! This is a journey that has only just begun. What we know thus far is the collected experiences from interacting with smart people, working very hard to help EA gain a seat at the acquisition table. This book is merely the result of collecting and organizing these experiences, feeding them into new contexts, and documenting the rewards. To continue this process, to continue to chase our running target, we will continue to learn from smart and hardworking people that make EA matter in the acquisition context. Therefore, we would like to extend an invitation to you to embark on your journey together with us. With all the nuances of EA and the complexity of the acquisition challenge, we share the drive to understand what makes EA at your company unique and your acquisition challenge different from others.

The best way to get ready for this future is to start putting EA into the acquisition process now. In a few years, when the need is apparent to everyone, it might be too late to start. The journey from scratch to a fully leveraged advanced EA capability that makes a difference in the acquisition process is measured in years, not months. It requires EA to understand acquisitions and the acquisition deal team to learn to work with EA, have mutual trust and a shared language, and it requires the establishment of new practices and new tools specifically chartered for the job. The good news is, however, that once you get going there are immediate benefits. Just having the documentation of your own IT landscape in place speeds up the process. That is still something. Something that matters to you and to your company. So, what are you waiting for?

We have written this book to help you on this journey. This is not a blueprint. It is not a recipe-like instruction for how to go about doing this. Every company is different, every acquisition is different, and the use of EA is bound to be specific in every single acquisition. But the cognitive keys and the practical guidelines form the foundation for you and your team to take on this challenge.

We hope that this book will be useful for you when you start your own journey towards putting EA into your acquisition process and unleash its full potential to define the future of your company!

Printed in the United States
By Bookmasters